PRAISE FOR AARON LIKENS AND

Finding Kansas

"Aaron Likens may be the most courageous, intelligent, and tenacious young man I have met in my long tenure in the mental health field. He is fiercely determined to better understand himself and the world around him, and he does us the great favor of sharing his journey of self-discovery, so profoundly touched by Asperger's syndrome. It is a condition that, before Aaron, led us to assume emotional insight and personal self disclosure might not be possible. We have much to learn from Aaron, and as he teaches us, our admiration, understanding, and respect for this brave young man, and all others affected by Asperger's syndrome, will grow."
—Keith Schafer, Ed.D.,
director, Missouri Department of Mental Health

"What Aaron has written provides a unique and unusual look into the cognitive processes involved in someone with Asperger's syndrome. Understanding these ideas and emotions are essential to provide a better understanding to autism spectrum disorders, including Asperger's syndrome. This will provide a unique contribution to scientific research as well as better awareness and understanding of people with this disorder."
—Alycia Halladay, Ph.D.

"[*Finding Kansas*] reveals depths of emotion, social comprehension, nuances of cognition and perception, and especially the potential for something close to 'recovery.' I believe it has the potential to change lives." —Mark A. ███████ ██., MA,
eword

FINDING KANSAS

Living and Decoding Asperger's Syndrome

Aaron Likens

A Perigee Book

A PERIGEE BOOK
Published by the Penguin Group
Penguin Group (USA) Inc.
375 Hudson Street, New York, New York 10014, USA

Penguin Group (Canada), 90 Eglinton Avenue East, Suite 700, Toronto, Ontario M4P 2Y3, Canada (a division of Pearson Penguin Canada Inc.) • Penguin Books Ltd., 80 Strand, London WC2R 0RL, England • Penguin Group Ireland, 25 St. Stephen's Green, Dublin 2, Ireland (a division of Penguin Books Ltd.) • Penguin Group (Australia), 250 Camberwell Road, Camberwell, Victoria 3124, Australia (a division of Pearson Australia Group Pty. Ltd.) • Penguin Books India Pvt. Ltd., 11 Community Centre, Panchsheel Park, New Delhi—110 017, India • Penguin Group (NZ), 67 Apollo Drive, Rosedale, Auckland 0632, New Zealand (a division of Pearson New Zealand Ltd.) • Penguin Books (South Africa) (Pty.) Ltd., 24 Sturdee Avenue, Rosebank, Johannesburg 2196, South Africa

Penguin Books Ltd., Registered Offices: 80 Strand, London WC2R 0RL, England

FINDING KANSAS

First edition: April 2012

Library of Congress Cataloging-in-Publication Data

Likens, Aaron.
Finding Kansas : living and decoding Asperger's syndrome / Aaron Likens. — 1st ed.
p. cm.
"A Perigee book."
ISBN 978-0-399-53733-2
1. Likens, Aaron. 2. Asperger's syndrome—Patients—United States—Biography.
3. Motorsports—United States—Biography. I. Title.
RC553.A88L55 2012
618.92'8588320092—dc23
[B]
2011043997

PRINTED IN THE UNITED STATES OF AMERICA

10 9 8 7 6 5 4 3 2

Most Perigee books are available at special quantity discounts for bulk purchases for sales promotions, premiums, fund-raising, or educational use. Special books, or book excerpts, can also be created to fit specific needs. For details, write: Special Markets, Penguin Group (USA) Inc., 375 Hudson Street, New York, New York 10014.

To Emily

FINDING KANSAS

CONTENTS

Contents

Contents

FOREWORD

I have been asked to write a brief description of my impression of the clinical value and importance of Aaron Likens's remarkable writings.

As a mental health professional who has specialized in the field of autistic spectrum disorders for nearly twenty years, and who worked with Aaron for more than a year, I am very pleased to see his remarkable writings in book form.

The only apt comparison I can make to Aaron's essays is the effect of Temple Grandin's first book, *Emergence*. Her personal account of the experience of autism was a revelation. It shattered many myths and previously accepted "facts" about autism. Her book permanently changed the previously limited understanding of autistic disorders.

I believe Aaron's writings have the same potential regarding Asperger's syndrome. (Interestingly, Aaron uses some of the same language to describe living with AS as

Dr. Grandin did, though he has never read her work.). He reveals depths of emotion, social comprehension, nuances of cognition and perception, and especially the potential for something close to "recovery." I believe it has the potential to change lives.

I think it is important to note that unlike most current books on the subject of Asperger's, this is not a "how-to" (treat symptoms, etc.) but a "how-do" book. It is Aaron's intensely personal journey, begun half unconsciously, its purpose emerging intuitively. The process has been self-healing, but the result, like many literary journeys, is that Aaron's story speaks to us all. When he came to realize its potential value to others, he unselfishly decided to share it.

His story is told in chronological order. It reflects the preoccupation with sameness, order, and predictability that is a hallmark to autism spectrum disorders.

Aaron has subjected himself to rigorous self-examination, using himself as the subject of this "study," a study of the nature and experience of Asperger's syndrome. He has bravely exposed us to his inner world. He queries himself relentlessly about the nature, meaning, and implications of his thoughts, feelings, and perceptions. In the course of this self-examination, he diligently applies logic, metaphor, analogy, and self-reflection in an attempt to understand his life.

This approach makes for a unique, self-made form of philosophical inquiry. When I say "self-made," I mean this literally, for Aaron reads very little and is completely unacquainted with the field of philosophy or any of its most notable contributors.

In the course of this personal odyssey, however, he becomes much more than a clinical study of Asperger's, for his personal queries eventually pose the same strenuous questions about the human experience that have challenged philosophers since antiquity: What is the meaning of our lives and actions? How do we reconcile our experience with that of others? Where does the truth lie? What is love? Does freedom equal love?

Aaron does not ask these questions casually or as a kind of intellectual game. He poses these earnestly, for he perceives this is the only place where his personal salvation may be found. To me this is one of the most fascinating and unique aspects of his writings.

Despite the cognitive inflexibility that is a hallmark of his condition, Aaron shares a tremendous amount of emotional honesty and clarity in these writings. He is often given to morbid recollection, doubt, and hopelessness, but there is also the zest and excitement of release, joy, and peace, and even moments of serenity and even blissful happiness.

At times you might feel that his outlook is bleak. But to travel with him through the dark nights, the deep valleys, the almost overwhelming disappointments, the crushing depression, and the moments of blissful happiness is worth it.

Where does he find this elusive happiness we all seek? One answer he discovers is in playing games such as Monopoly. In asking himself why this is so, he finds compelling answers regarding his Asperger's mind-set; the fact that games have clear rules that temper the "unpredictable," that "there's no better feeling than the unpredictability of a game set with predictable rules." He sees he is temporarily "free of my mind . . . of all the other mental anguish . . . the chains that make me overanalyze life, the critical mind . . . The real world and my world coincide, and happiness is found through the medium of the game."

But a more comprehensive, even profound insight arises from Aaron's study of himself. It is an existential, even spiritual observation that "within rules comes knowledge of boundaries and limitation . . . [that] I am free because there are limits."

Finding Kansas offers readers a glimpse into the deeply thoughtful, insightful, and infinitely curious young man I have had the privilege to work with, and who has taught me a great deal about his condition and the mysteries of the human mind and heart.

I find hope in one of Aaron's many pithy aphorisms, which he has stated many times in my office: "The rule that saved my life was the rule that there is an exception to every rule."

—MARK A. CAMERON, Ph.D., MA
ST. LOUIS, MISSOURI

A FEW WORDS ABOUT MY SON

"Aaron doesn't socialize real well with the other kids," the preschool teacher told me. "But I think it is probably due to his high intelligence."

Year after year that was what I heard, and year after year I believed it. In fact, it was rather a proud moment at every parent-teacher conference when the teacher would say—and I could tell it was coming—"I think it is probably due to his high intelligence."

Aaron *was* intelligent. He knew the alphabet by the time he was eighteen months. By the time he was three, he could spell all the words on his Speak & Spell. During his fifth year he got his first Monopoly game and was the banker. Before his sixth birthday I stopped playing Monopoly with him, because I always lost. Before he was seven, he taught himself the multiplication table after he asked me what the "x" meant in one of his sister's math problems. Boy, oh boy, was I ever a proud papa.

There was one big problem: Aaron didn't want to go to school, especially if there was the threat of severe weather. He also didn't want to go to school if the sun was shining; or if it was Monday, Tuesday, Wednesday, Thursday, or Friday. I think from the second grade on he missed more days in the school year than he attended. Yet, he was always one of the top students in the class. Oh, did I tell you it was probably due to his high intelligence?

As a Lutheran pastor, much of my time was spent "saving" the world. I didn't really notice the lack of friends in Aaron's life. I really didn't think it was a problem that at six months, when most children start taking solid food, his mouth wouldn't work to swallow. When he was two and spoke no intelligible words, I figured it was because his older brother and sister did most of the talking for him.

I could go on and on about the "whens," but I won't. Suffice it to say there were so many things I didn't notice, or chose to deny, or took pride in—"I think it's probably due to his high intelligence"—I didn't see any "real" problem, but then, I never noticed dirty socks, either.

At one point, because of his fear and unwillingness to go to school, I called the mental health–care provider that served pastors of the Lutheran Church—Missouri Synod. They gave me the name of a psychiatrist in Clayton, Missouri, a suburb of St. Louis. During the one-hour visit, the venerable doctor said Aaron would probably grow up to be a serial killer. Needless to say, this was not a prognosis I was going to accept.

Six months later another noted child psychiatrist in the

St. Louis area said he thought Aaron suffered from PDD-NOS, Pervasive Developmental Disorder—Not Otherwise Specified. As Aaron, his mother, and I sat there, I asked, "My oldest son had ADD, and we took hope in the fact that great people like Thomas Edison reportedly had ADD. Is there anyone like that concerning this PDD thing?"

"Oh yes," the doctor quickly replied. "Ted Kaczynski, the Unabomber."

Instills a lot of hope, don't you think?

In 2000, Aaron's mother and I divorced. Up to that point, much of my relationship with Aaron had been spent playing games, going to races, or racing go-karts. I remarried in 2002, and the next year Aaron moved in with me and his stepmother, Mary. She and her son, Michael, saw many things that I hadn't. They didn't know what the problem was, but they knew for sure there was one.

It wasn't until Aaron was twenty years old that I read an article in a Sunday news magazine that talked about savant traits in children with autism. Aaron wasn't one of those math wizards, nor did he know the batting average of every baseball player in the history of the world. He did know a lot about auto racing, but the characteristics that stood out the most were his eye-to-hand coordination and his reflexes.

I did some research on the Internet and read about PDD-NOS, autism, and Asperger's. I began to realize that I had bought into the lie of "It is probably due to his high intelligence." Mary was right. There was a problem. Aaron was intelligent, but he was also a unique member of the autism spectrum.

I called the Judevine Center in St. Louis, a most noted organization that works with ASD children from evaluation to treatment, and scheduled an evaluation. Prior to making that appointment I spent a great deal of time talking with Aaron about my conclusions. As I shared with him the characteristics of Asperger's that I had discovered, he kept asking me, "But what does this mean?" (A good Lutheran question.) I didn't have a complete answer, but I did tell him whatever we found out from the evaluation, progress and change would be difficult.

As the day neared for the appointment, Aaron told me that he didn't want to talk much to whoever would be doing the assessment. I said, "Why don't you write a short essay and call it 'I Wish' and describe how you wish your life was."

That was the beginning of what you are about to read. Since then, Aaron has continued to write in order to survive. It has been the most therapeutic treatment he has ever received. The amazing thing is that he did it all himself. What he has gained is invaluable, and I believe that what others will discover about ASD will be priceless.

I believe that like the cryptographers who cracked the code of the Enigma machine used by the Germans, Aaron has begun the process of decoding the enigma of Asperger's syndrome.

Among the many misconceptions about Asperger's that Aaron debunks is a lack of empathy. As he describes in "A Friend Gone," he struggles to understand an immense, almost overwhelming sense of loss. He brings a similar depth of honesty and insight to the subjects of time, memory, uncertainty, the pain of social interactions, relationships gone wrong—and even the loss of an old soda can. He also shares insights into finding joy and comfort—what he calls Kansas—in the thrill of racing, the art of race-flagging, the comforting world of rule-based games, and the emotional respite and relief that comes with something most of us dread: airport layovers. Perhaps most important, he presents a new way of explaining his condition, calling it a situational handicap. His concept of Kansas—a place where he feels calm, capable, and whole—has even been adopted by some top professionals in the autism world.

It is important to understand that Aaron doesn't present Asperger's syndrome as a set of symptoms. He digs far beneath the intellectual, academic, medical, and psychological definitions and offers insights into not *what* Asperger's is but rather *how* it is to live with it.

Please keep in mind that this book was not written in order to write a book. It was written in order to survive. These writings expose the heart and emotions of a young man who has been willing to share the thoughts and feelings that most of us are afraid to acknowledge. His journey of exploration is about to become yours.

Bon voyage.

—JIM LIKENS
ST. LOUIS, MISSOURI

------ A NOTE FROM DAD ------

At the start of some of Aaron's essays, you will find a short introductory note from me, offering a bit of context to Aaron's observations. It is my hope that his insights will lead to a better understanding of Asperger's among parents, teachers, clinicians, and therapists—as well as children and adults who are themselves on the autism spectrum.

The Best Day

Like most children with AS, Aaron had a special interest, an interest that put his life on the edge every time he participated in it.

In his first college course, English Comp 101, he had to write an essay titled "The Best Day." From that day on, the quote below became the essence of his life.

"I've wanted to race since I was five years old.

That's plan A for my life. There is no plan B."

It was a cool, humid April morning. It was five o'clock in the morning, still two hours before I had to get up, but I just couldn't sleep and was counting down the minutes until I had to go. My dad was shocked to see me up when he awoke, but if you've waited for something all your life, you wouldn't be able to sleep, either.

So where were we going that had me so nervous that I felt

like one of those knots you can't get out of your shoelaces? We were headed to Widman Raceway for my first go-kart race. I was just twelve years old, but it felt like two hundred years waiting to get my chance to race. On the drive to the track, I began to ponder how I got to this opportunistic point in time where I'd get the chance to start what I had envisioned myself doing since I was a little kid.

Growing up in Indianapolis, where they have a little thing known as the Indianapolis 500, and being exposed to drivers and fast cars from my dad taking me to the practice runs, I got the itch to race at an early age.

It was a long road indeed, but now all my waiting was about to be put to rest. As I signed in for the race, the woman who handed me the release form asked, "So, today's your first race?"

"Yes, and I can't wait!" I said.

She responded, "Well, then, enjoy yourself, have fun, and don't worry how you do."

Enjoy myself? I wasn't here to just have fun and enjoy myself, I was here to win or at least finish in the top five.

We pulled into our pit spot and unloaded the van. After a few practice sessions, the race director met with all the rookie drivers to go through racing procedures. He explained the flags and how the race day would work. There'd be two heat races and then a feature race. He told us that for our first three race weekends, we'd have to start in the back of the pack for safety reasons. He then said, "And remember, it's your first race, don't be concerned with how you do, just have fun." Everyone kept saying that, as if we had no chance of finishing in the top five positions. It was driving me up a wall. I knew I was good, at least I always won in the video games I played, but why did everyone count us out?

Twenty minutes passed after the driver's meeting, and then it was time for my race to commence. We started our motors and waited. As I waited eagerly for the race that preceded us to finish, my mind began racing at a ferocious pace. I thought about the insurance forms I had read and how serious injury or even death can occur. I thought about what my mom said as I left my house: "Now, Aaron, whatever you do, just don't get hurt. You hear me, *don't* get hurt." I finally realized that this was a dangerous activity. I mean, hurling your body in a moving projectile at speeds in excess of forty miles per hour without a seat belt or roll cage two inches off the ground isn't the safest sport a twelve-year-old could be competing in. My mind continued to race around like a dog chasing its tail until I got the signal to roll.

As soon as I started to pick up speed, every thought about how dangerous this was vanished quicker than lasagna fed to Garfield. We did one warm-up lap, and then it was time to take the green. I was starting fifteen out of seventeen, and as we rolled off the final corner, the green flag was displayed, and we were off. That start was one of the most nerve-racking moments in my life, because there was a kart behind me, a kart beside me, and thirteen karts in front of me. As we entered turns one and two, a couple of karts in front of me tangled and spun. *Oh no*, I said to myself, *I'm going to get hurt right away. What's my mom going to think?* I pulled off a great move and avoided the two pirou-etting karts and in the process advanced to eighth place.

By lap four out of ten, I had moved up to second and was challenging for the lead. I went for the lead going into turn one; the announcer, the late traffic helicopter pilot Allen Barklage, was enthusiastic to say the least. "And that's Aaron Likens challenging the leader, going into turn one. Side by side they go, and *oh*! They've touched, and Aaron's going to spin, whoa, he saved it. How did he save that? I can't believe this is only Aaron's first race." I didn't quite pull the pass off, but I had another chance on the final lap. Allen commented, "Coming out of the final turn, Aaron to the inside for the lead—nope, not going to get the win, but a valiant effort for just his first race."

As I pulled off the track and onto the scales, everyone was giving me the thumbs-up sign and clapping. The feel-ing was simply indescribable. Think of pure happiness and multiply that by ten. The look of disbelief on my dad's face was priceless. I knew he thought I'd do decently, but I don't exactly think he was expecting me to touch side pods with the leader of the race. As we lifted the kart onto the scale and weighed, I asked my dad, "How'd I do?" He didn't reply, which for me was the best response. He was in a state of total shock.

The following race wasn't as eventful, and I didn't do as well, finishing fifth. Still impressive being my first race, but at the same time disappointing since I started off with a second; I was hoping to pull off a win.

It was getting late in the day. The sun was now in the

western part of the sky, and clouds had begun to hesitantly drift into the area. The aroma of kart exhaust was in the air. With just about ten minutes to go until my race, I asked my dad, "How do you think I'll do in this final race?"

"You'll do just fine," he replied.

"Are you sure?"

"Absolutely," he said calmly.

It turned out I did do well, finishing fourth in the feature for an excellent day overall. As we were heading home, I asked my dad, "So, Dad, how'd I do today?"

"Well," he responded, "let's just say you've got it. Someday, you're going to win the Indianapolis 500."

Wow, I thought, *maybe I actually do have it*. And in that moment, I decided that racing was going to be my career choice, and if I got as far as I had gotten today, nothing was going to stop me from my dream.

I found where I was meant to be.

Emily

That day I told Aaron, "Let's just say you've got it. Someday, you're going to win the Indianapolis 500," was, as I look back, one of the saddest days of my life.

You see, and you will learn from Aaron, when something happens the first time, it always has to be like that. If your dad says you're going to win the Indy 500, it's not a question of "if"; it's a question of, "Are we there yet?"

I implanted in Aaron's mind the reality that it would happen. It hasn't. It has created great pain and sorrow for both of us.

I sent to him to racing schools in Las Vegas and Tampa. He was one of the fastest students they'd ever had. We raced go-karts for six years and then abandoned them for a ride in the big time. We had a deal with an ARCA team, a race series just under the ranks of NASCAR, and it went sour when we found out the team had an illegal car. I talked to sprint car owners, and if Aaron had had track time, he would have had a ride. He didn't have track time. He had a chance to race in the training series for the Champ Car Series, and I didn't have sixty thousand dollars. He had everything needed for Plan A except for one thing: a dad with a million bucks.

But if we had landed that ARCA ride, or sprint ride, or if I had had sixty thousand dollars, this book would not exist. You see, how Aaron dealt with his disappointments was to write. He had plenty of disappointments. Many nights I sat up with him while he cried. Many days I hated myself for not being able to deliver on that statement that took on the power of a promise: "Let's just say you've got it. Someday, you're going to win the Indianapolis 500."

Things really do work out. Most of the time, however, it's not like we think they should. But then, since when did God start asking his creation how to do things?

The disappointment of not getting a big-time ride was a daily reality for Aaron. There was one bright spot, though: Emily (not her real name). It was Emily who started Aaron on this journey of writing.

This is where Aaron begins.

THE BEGINNING

When I was fifteen and being homeschooled, my mom thought it would be good if I got involved in some type of physical activity. She took me bowling and the lady at the counter asked if I wanted to join a league. Wow. That was great. I would have a chance to compete every week. That day, unbeknownst to me, would put into motion a series of events that would change my life.

For the next two years I bowled in two leagues, and I also worked at the bowling alley twice a week. At the start of the new season, I discovered I was paired with a girl named Emily.

Emily arrived one minute after the start of practice (remember that statement), and I didn't recognize her at first. I finally realized it was her by the way she threw the ball. To say the least, it was weird. Okay, enough about bowling physics.

Throughout the ten-minute practice session I didn't talk. As practice finished up, she finally said, "Hi, I'm Emily," and I replied with a nervous, "Hi, I'm Aaron."

I usually don't talk, but we started talking about dogs, cats, school, and racing. There wasn't a silent moment. I decided to show up for week two.

Week two was as talkative as the first, and it was that week that Emily mentioned she was hoping to be put on my team.

It was the fourth week. It took me two and a half games but I nervously asked for her email address. I was shocked when she gave it to me.

It was about mid-October when we scheduled our first *unofficial* date. Unofficial, because it would be illegal, in her mom's eye, to date me because I was only seventeen and she was nineteen, and that most certainly would lead to some sort of jail time, like those tags on pillows. Whatever.

I asked her to go cosmic bowling on a Friday night. I showed up an hour early and was waiting for her. Nine thirty came and passed and there was no Emily. Finally, she called the alley and told me that her mom wouldn't let her go because there was a 10 percent chance of freezing rain and/or sleet. If only I had realized what that night would mean in the future.

The next week the weather was fine and she showed up five minutes after bowling started. I asked her why she couldn't veto her mom's idea. She didn't have an answer.

When bowling ended, Emily drove me home and I asked if she would like to come in and play the NES (Nintendo) game *The Three Stooges*. I was shocked when she said she owned one. It's quite a rare game.

We played for quite a while and had a great time. She left and called me when she got back home. I was quick to memorize both her home and cell phone numbers. The numbers became as much a part of her in my mind as her actual being.

By the end of October I needed to know the "official" status of our relationship. I called Emily to find out if we were actually *dating*. It took me more than two hours to actually ask the question, but she was so quick to play the age card. "What? You're two years younger than me." I figured that came from her mother, but would the police immediately have arrived at her house if she said yes?

I was devastated. For some deep reason, I needed that *official* status to feel secure.

Thanksgiving came and went, and we were still going cosmic bowling and talking on the phone even without having official status. Then Christmas Eve came, and I returned late from my sister's house in Indianapolis. I called her and again, I asked, "What's the official status?"

Maybe I am too caught up in the whole needing-to-know-what's-going-on thing, but I just wanted, no, *needed* to know. Again, the age card was played.

The first week of January Emily took me to Olive Garden. It was there that finally, yes, finally, *official status* was secured. If she had said no, I was going to walk.

A couple of Sundays later the Daytona 500 ran and she came over to my house to watch the race. It was lap 173 when the "Daytona Big One" happened. Fox broke into the commercial, and the scene was that of a smoldering mass of what used to be twenty-six race cars.

My dad was working so I immediately called him to tell him what had happened. As I watched the replays I described them for my dad. I then hung up.

Ten minutes later the red flag was rescinded and the yellow came back out. I called my dad again. He then made a terrifying prediction: "Earnhardt is going to crash in turn four of the final lap." I said, "Okay, whatever," and then went on watching the final laps.

When the white flag came out (signifying one lap to go), and as the field came through turns three and four, I saw in the corner of the screen a black car go to the apron and the announcer screamed, "Oh, *big* crash!"

At the same time my mom and Emily were talking about some irrelevant topic, but I knew that this crash was bad. I quickly called my dad and told him what had happened. My mom and Emily paid no attention to the seriousness of the situation, and Emily had a weird look on her face.

About an hour later came the official word that, indeed, Dale Earnhardt was dead. I maintained my composure for probably thirty minutes, and then I lost it. Emily was there for me, and she just held me as I cried away.

The last sentence of the paragraph above would sound like it would be quite the bonding experience, but sadly that was ruined ten minutes after she left. When she got home, she called me and yelled and asked why I was on the phone with my dad so much. Maybe she couldn't understand that I actually wanted to talk to my dad. If she was so mad that I was on the phone, why didn't she just say something then and there? I asked her that, but I was getting used to the fact that I wouldn't get an answer.

The routine for the next three months was the same. But during this time I started learning more about her. Here's a quote from my journal at the time: "I don't know if I really like Emily. She is so odd. But I can't say good-bye. Oh, I am so trapped, what can I do?"

What could I do? I was trapped. Even in good times, I don't think I really cared for her. Was I missing Linda, my previous girlfriend? Did I just not like the girl? I don't know the answer to those questions, but I did know I didn't want to lose her. A true trap it was.

Jump ahead eight months . . .

THE BEGINNING OF THE END

There was to be a kart race in Quincy, Illinois, and Emily said she would drive up. She would have been twenty-one at the time. She called me at two a.m. on the morning of the day we were supposed to leave and said she wasn't going.

What hurt the most was that, in the eleventh hour, I was told she wouldn't be there. Sunday was actually a washout, but it still hurt that she wasn't there. When I got back, she told me if she had to do it over again she would've gone, because she understood how much her being there meant to me.

Well, guess what? She would get her chance. One month later a race was scheduled for Springfield, Illinois. She said she would go. But guess what? If you said in the eleventh hour in the middle of the night she called me and told me that she might get lost and such, you win the prize. The chance was there, but history repeated itself. This time it hurt twice as much because she promised that if she had to do it over again, the result would be different.

That was the first of many times I broke up with her. I think I did it just to get a reaction from her. I never knew how she felt about me. Well, she was just like, "Okay," and went on talking about school. I got back with her officially the next day, and things went back to normal, or rather what was passing for normal.

Over the next several months I traveled to Road America in Elkhart Lake, Wisconsin, took an advance course at the Derek Daly Racing Academy in Las Vegas, and tested with a Formula Mazda team in Benton Harbor, Michigan.

This would be the first time I'd be in a legitimate race car. The sense of acceleration was something I had never felt before. Like many people with Asperger's, I'm very sensitive to the slightest changes in my physical environment. I'm telling you all this because, trust me, I'm building to something.

The sensation of deceleration when I hit the brakes was so great that breathing seemed impossible. The shoulder belts felt like they were crushing my chest. The sensations were so uncomfortable that I thought my racing career and dreams were going to die that day.

I had my first on-track session, and with less than twenty-five minutes of on-track time, I was just about a second off the official track record and five seconds faster than the previous weekend's pole time.

I made a phone call.

"Hey, Emily, how are you?" I asked.

"Umm, fine and yourself?" she replied.

"Well, I was just about a second off the official track record and I reached one hundred and—"

Just then she cut me off and then said, "Look, Aaron, I'm on break and I'm sipping a soda; do you think you could call me back?"

Call her back? Sipping a soda? What's wrong with this picture?

Jump ahead a few months—now it's early June. Due to a conversation I overheard between my brother and mom I moved out of the house, and in with my dad and step-mother. At the same time, my sixteen-year-old dog, Missy the Maltese, was on her way out. When she made the move to my dad's she lost bladder control. So the next morning I calmly told my dad that it was her time. Not a tear was shed until my dad cried; then I felt his pain. Add to that, Emily didn't understand a darn thing, and things were bound to get messy.

Four months after moving, I got the chance of a lifetime to be a guest instructor at the Derek Daly Racing Academy. I would be relocating to Vegas for a while. At the same time I started taking an antidepressant. The side effects were masked by the freedom I experienced in Las Vegas. But before I even left St. Louis, disaster struck.

HERE COMES THE END

Emily wasn't that pleased that I was going to Vegas for racing school. It wasn't that she would miss me. She became snooty when I told her how much I was going to get paid per day. You see, she had a college degree and felt she should get paid more than Mr. GED.

As my departure neared, we agreed to spend the entire Sunday together. We would watch a NASCAR race, a Formula One (F1) race, and eat at our favorite pizza place. It was going to be the best going-away day.

About halfway into Talladega, she said she was going to have to go home early to help clean out her *mom's* closet. What? So she left early, ruining the remainder of the day. It was going to get worse. With twenty laps to go in the race I knew there would be a big wreck. I tried to call her but her home phone just went to voice mail, and her cell phone just rang. I tried calling every half hour.

The big wreck happened, but I still hadn't heard from her. Five hours later she calls me and asks sternly, "Why in the world did you call my cell phone twenty-one times?" I said I wanted her to watch the finish of the race and told her I feared for her safety. This would seem to be a boyfriend concerned for his girlfriend's well-being, wouldn't it? She didn't see it that way and fired back, "Aaron, you need to quit being so darn possessive!"

Whoa! Me? Possessive? That would be one word that never would describe my relationship with her.

Two days more and I would be away from it all. Or so I thought. My new cell phone was delayed in the mail, so I had decided to spend the day with Emily before I left. One thing stood in the way—her job. She wouldn't take the day off. That hurt so badly because, as I've said before, the *job* held precedence over her boyfriend of more than three years.

That evening she called me and said that *if she had to do it all over again,* she would have done it differently. Sound familiar? Well, guess what? The cell phone was delayed again. So on Friday she would have her chance to do it all over again. But again, she couldn't say no to her job.

That was the dagger that opened the wound that could not be healed. While my time at the racing school in Vegas was such a joy, at the same time I had the albatross of Emily on my mind. Every time I talked to her I just wanted to know why she couldn't see me before I left. All I wanted was something—whether it was because she just couldn't say good-bye or that she didn't really like me. Whatever it was, I wanted to know something. Anything.

This was the enigma with Emily: in many cases, there was nothing. She did say, however, "Well, I said that [I'd do it differently] because I didn't think I was going to get the chance and saying that would make you feel better. I could never say no to my job. They might talk about me while I was gone."

Whatever.

THE END AND BEYOND

When I got back, the side effects of the antidepressant were getting worse. Granted, they were so gradual I didn't notice them, but they made me different, more impulsive. And on that fateful Christmas, I broke up with her for what would be the final time. That's the second worst thing I have ever done to somebody. To do it on Christmas is almost inexcusable. To do it by text message is even worse. To think she cared was dumb. Regardless of the circumstances, Christmas should not be a breakup day. Right before I pressed the send button on that text message I was "official" with Emily: the nanosecond after, it was all over.

I instantly missed her, and I tried to get back to being official with her the next day. No such luck this time.

I spent the first third of the following year trying to recover the relationship, but I think she was extracting her revenge by saying, "I don't know. I just need time." I was diagnosed with Asperger's two weeks after I broke up with her. And once I told her, she seemed to use its symptoms to hurt me.

One night during bowling she was hinting that she might want to be "official" again. But just as the stock market can change in a heartbeat, so, too, did her mind. She handed me the cruelest words I think I could be handed: "Aaron, you have Asperger's, and I don't think anyone would want a relationship with someone with that!" One word summarized that: *devastating*.

I wouldn't hear from again her until December 31. On the ride back from Indy on New Year's Eve, I simply sent her a text message asking if she forgave me. She called and asked what that meant. This was the first time in nearly six months I had heard her voice, and I needed to hear it so badly. I told her I just wanted to know if she forgave me for breaking up on Christmas, and she said yes. Then we talked like we weren't apart all those months. Thirty to forty minutes later she said she had to eat and that she would call me right back. Well, that was about forty days ago, and she still hasn't called back.

So now, I don't understand the emotional side of my mind. Emily was pretty inept when it came to a relationship and emotions. So why do I hurt so badly not having her? Is it simply because I have no one else?

But with all the problems and meltdowns we had, why do I yearn to hear her voice? I miss her and there's nothing I can do to reverse it. There is no reset button. There is no Ctrl + Z.

I have to live with the vacuum of Emily for the rest of my life. Even though I didn't care for her, I miss her. And there is no logic in it. You could say it was all about a safety net and routine, but no routine is safe enough for me to live with it and be miserable.

The thing that hurts, and this also applies to my previous relationship with Linda, is will I ever hear from them again? Will I ever see them again? Will I hear their voices? Or do I have to wait until the post-life show in heaven? Today they are only blurs in my memory. The only physical memory is their numbers: *phone numbers*.

Linda

----- A NOTE FROM DAD -----

Although Aaron wrote about Emily first, there was another
girl. The chance encounter was like two ships colliding in the
night. It took him a long time to recover from the impact.

There is no name that has more power over me than the
name that is written above. You might not understand now,
but you will learn how this one name has haunted more
than 25 percent of my life.

It was July of 1999. My dad and I were in Minneapolis to
work at a convention. My dad was going to put on a mini
concert at the booth he shared with his video distributor,
and to promote it I came up with the idea of becoming a
human billboard. After about an hour of walking around I
decided to take a rest at the booth.

As I was sitting there, I noticed this girl standing near another exhibit. I thought I recognized her from my church in St. Louis. She started walking toward me and asked, "What in the name of Sam Hill are you wearing?" I replied that I had to help my dad raise awareness of his concert, so I was willing to go to the bottom of the barrel to help out the cause. At that moment, I still thought this person was someone I went to church with, so I replied to her questions, much out of the ordinary for me. Five minutes passed and I finally looked at her name tag, and the hometown was Baltimore. I didn't know this girl after all! So to whom was I talking? I would never have the nerve to talk to any girl because I felt that doing so was somehow illegal. I instantly started giving one-word answers.

Then she asked the question that would change my life forever: "Would you like to play Uno?" You'll understand the importance of that question later. I firmly said yes to that game of Uno.

And boy, did we play Uno. We must have played for two hours, and all the while we were talking about various topics. She asked my age and I told her sixteen. I didn't ask her hers, but she volunteered that she, too, was sixteen. It took a while, but I became a chatterbox as we shared stories of being a pastor's kid (her dad was a pastor, too) and then, for the first time in my life, I actually started asking the first question. That was strange for me, but I cared about her answer. This is important because until this day I never thought a girl would ever want to talk to me for any reason whatsoever, and I never cared what anyone outside of family had to say. So for the first time that rule I lived by was shattered.

Three hours had passed; then she remembered she had to meet her mom somewhere in the hall. She jumped up quickly but said she'd return at some point in time. How long would that be? I went from experiencing something I never thought possible to losing it in less than five seconds. But there was hope. She left her backpack. That backpack was more than a backpack; it represented my lifeline to this person called Linda who took the time of day to talk to me. But where was she?

I waited for two hours. I scanned every girl in the crowd of thousands. Suddenly I heard a familiar voice that said, "Ready for a rematch?" It was her, and she was ready for some more Uno and I was quite ready to talk to her again.

After twelve or so hands, we walked and talked for another two hours. We got an ice cream cone. We were two bored kids at an old women's convention who'd happened to cross paths.

It was nearing five p.m., and the convention was closing for the day, so I asked Linda if I would see her the next day, and she said certainly. With my negative outlook, I wondered if that was a true statement.

Linda had shattered my worldview and the view of myself. My dad kept trying to talk about the NASCAR Pepsi 400 that would be run the next night. But Linda was the only thing I could think about. Would she be at the booth the next day?

The next day, July 3, would change my life. The Pepsi 400

would haunt me. It all began with a stellar sunrise and our arrival at the convention center. I began scanning the crowd. Would Linda appear? It was about ten a.m. and there she was. My cautious sense of optimism had been fulfilled.

We picked up where we left off: talking about the downfall of Western civilization, the knucklehead who sat in the Oval Office, and so many other topics. We went upstairs to play Uno again, we had lunch together, and we took a long walk. It was on this walk that Linda attempted, I think, to hold my hand. Now, understand, I try to avoid physical contact with people, and second, unless she had grabbed my hand, I would have no clue what someone's intentions were. Well, I do know she tried, because later she would tell me so.

It was now about two p.m.; time was ticking. What time, you ask? Remember the race that haunts me? That's what was ticking. In order to make it back to the hotel, we would have to leave between five and five thirty p.m. I didn't try to hide why I had to leave to Linda. Looking back on it, I was quite stupid. My dad had to leave for St. Louis the next day, and for me Independence Day would have a new meaning. In the end, what should have been a celebration of America's independence would become a day of imprisonment.

Speaking of independence, for the first time in my life I was free: free from the negative self-talk that lived in my head every day, and free from the thought of whether I was likeable. Yes, for me I surely thought this was Independence Day.

It took a while, but I asked her if she had an email address. She did, and I also got her phone number and Yahoo! Messenger tag. I kept that sheet of paper for the longest time.

The time to leave had arrived. My dad had already loaded the van and was headed around to the front of the convention center. This was it. After all the games of Uno, after all the exploring and talking and sharing of emotions, this was it—the hardest good-bye I have ever known. Leaving Linda, who I had only known for twelve hours, was the hardest thing I ever had to do.

For two hours we had sat outside and just talked, both knowing what lay ahead. She later told me that she tried to hint that I should kiss her while we sat there, but I was totally oblivious to that.

For the first time in my life I held a girl's hand, and suddenly, with one painful hug, she walked away and disappeared into the mass of people. For some strange reason I knew this would be the last time I would ever see this girl who changed my life. As I was walking out of the convention center, buckets of tears were just waiting to erupt.

That race, the Pepsi 400 at Daytona, is normally one of the best races of the year. I thought it more important to watch that race than spend more time with Linda. And fittingly, to show me where my priorities should have been, the race just sucked.

Lap after lap, I realized that I may never see Linda again. I tried to convince my dad to stay for the last day of the convention, but he said it would be practically impossible to find her among thousands unless we had made arrangements to meet somewhere. Plus, he needed to get back to St. Louis for work.

But wait, I had her email address and phone number. I could email her as soon as I got home, right? Wrong! Her grandma or aunt lived fifteen miles outside Minneapolis, and she wouldn't be home in Baltimore for another two weeks . . . two long weeks.

I had given her my email address and Yahoo! Messenger screen name and one night, out of the blue, Miss_nom_ de_2000 appeared on my screen with the message, *Hi, remember me?* Remember her? I had waited all two hundred eighty–plus hours for this moment. I was once again was connected with Linda. We talked for so many hours that night. Or rather we didn't talk, we "chatted."

As we were wrapping up our chat, she mentioned she was going to Panama with this Christian group for a mission trip. Little did I know what this trip would bring. Would she be safe in Panama? Would she still talk to me when she got back?

Just as had happened forty-five days earlier, a random name appeared on my computer screen, and again was the message, *Hello, remember me?* It was Linda, but where was Miss_nom_de_2000? Now it was warrior_2000. I almost cried; I had become so attached to her first screen name that it was almost like losing her again. If only I had realized that it was the beginning of the end of losing her.

She explained that she had changed her screen name to better reflect her dedication to Jesus. She also, out of the blue, laid down the rules that were to be followed if we were ever to meet again. Among them was no dating unless someone else was present.

It was now early October, and again a random name appeared on my computer screen; this time it was on_fire_ with_god. Linda said that her new name was a better statement of how dedicated she was to God. I didn't fully understand what was happening, but in time I would.

October 31, 1999, would mark the beginning of the formation of a black hole in my life.

There was series of tragic events that created the initial black dwarf star: the Littleton school massacre; leaving Oklahoma City the day before the F5 killer tornado; missing an IRL race at Charlotte where several people were killed in the section where I would have been seated.

So now, on October 31, the black dwarf star started to collapse. It wasn't something Linda said but rather a race on television. In that race IRL driver Greg Moore was killed instantly in a horrible crash when he hit an inside wall.

Why is this important? I couldn't see it coming. I wasn't prepared. I can usually watch a race and know a crash is going to happen before it does. So it wasn't the death that hurt; it was the suddenness of it all.

One week later, I saw the movie that brought about the formation of the black hole. *Life Is Beautiful* had to have been the most depressing film I ever watched, but it made me realize something. We could die on any day at any second. So I emailed Linda that night saying how much I cared about her and that I hoped I would know her the rest of my life.

I heard the Yahoo! Messenger alert. I was shocked. The reply was a cold, almost hostile response. It was something along the lines that such thoughts were ungodly. Earlier she had sent me five photos of herself, and a card that stated she was so thankful to God that we had met, and that she hoped I would be in her life forever. Why was it now a crime for me to want to know her?

In late November 1999, my dad and I were headed to Oklahoma City for Thanksgiving. And much like the premonition that my dad had about the 2001 Daytona 500 (Dale Earnhardt hitting the wall on the last lap), I predicted that this would be a bumpy trip because of storms. My dad had a meeting with a singer in Branson, Missouri, and as we walked out of her theater, I warned him, "I smell *big* storms." Boy, was I right.

Three hours later, somewhere in northeastern Oklahoma, we hit it. There were reported tornadoes everywhere. I believed I was going to die. We traveled to the next exit, and the first thing I did was call Linda.

It was eight thirty p.m. CST, which made it nine thirty p.m. in Baltimore. The phone rang and her dad picked up. As soon as I asked if Linda was there, he responded harshly, "Do you know what *time* it is?" What time is it? I'm about to die, and he's concerned about time! He finally agreed that I could talk to her for five minutes.

I needed to hear her voice before I died. (Sorry for the drama, but it sure seemed like it was going to happen.) She started out by telling me that it was "quite inappropriate" that I called her.

I replied with, "Umm, Linda, I might die here tonight."

"Why would you call me?" she countered.

I said, "Because you know more about me than anyone else, and above all you're my best friend and I trust you." That was enough, and she dropped the whole inappropriate thing, or so I thought.

She prayed with me and asked God to keep me safe, and that obviously worked, and then five minutes were up and she had to go. The massive storm had passed, so we decided to forge on to Oklahoma City. Somewhere between there and Tulsa we ran into another storm. This time we were out in the open and there was no shelter. My dad parked under an overpass. I thought I was afraid before, but under that overpass I experienced true mortal fear.

You know the feeling right before a plane takes off? Well, that was what my dad's van felt like. The wind sounded just like traveling in a high-speed race car. It was roaring. There were lightning flashes every half second. It wasn't a matter of if I would die, it was matter of when. I came to the conclusion that this was probably it, and I reached into the glove compartment and took out my name tag from Minneapolis. It was the only connection I had with the one person outside my family that I would miss if I died. I held on to that so tightly that if we had been blown into the air, that name tag would have stayed in my frozen hand.

Just to let you know, I didn't die. We finally arrived at my great-aunt's house (ironically her name is . . . Linda). I immediately got my dad's laptop out to email Linda and tell her that, by the grace of God, I was still alive. But guess what? She had already emailed me saying how wrong it was for me to call her at "that time of night."

So the middle stanza of the end had been set. She seemed more concerned about her new religious conviction than my near-death experience. She was ending emails with tag lines such as *doing God's work* and *wrapped up in God's blessings*. It seemed like she was using God as a wall between us.

On that memorable New Year's Eve, we talked on the phone for probably three hours. I thought we were working things out—though I could tell that her new belief system was taking more control of her by the day. I couldn't see it coming, but the final episode of our relationship was beginning on the Friday before the 2000 Daytona 500.

It was the first NASCAR truck race at Daytona. Geoff Bodine hit a wall and his truck exploded into a fireball, sending it tumbling like a toy car. While in the air, another truck hit him, launching him into the air again. In the end, Geoff suffered only minor injuries and was back racing just seven months later, but the damage was final for me.

What damage, you ask? Just like Greg Moore's crash and death, I once more arrived at the death-at-any-moment state of mind. I am perfectly comfortable with my own death, but it's the death of those around me that I fear. And besides that, Linda's involvement with this new group was getting to be too much for me.

So in February I sent her a terminal message, expressing my concerns about her distorted religious beliefs. This would be the last communication with her that I was sure she had read.

I did get a response. It wasn't a defense; it was a statement of fact. It ended with, *Have a good life, and please never try and contact me again.*

What had I done? The person who changed my life was gone. The one who showed me that happiness could be found outside of a race car was gone.

To date I have had no communication with her whatsoever. I tried to contact her a few times, to ask forgiveness, but to no avail. I emotionally punish myself every day because I have no one to blame but myself for losing contact with the most important person in my life.

What would make this better for me? I've looked for that answer for nearly five years now. It's been half a decade and the wounds just keeps getting deeper. For me there was and is no closure.

Later I realized that I hadn't seen her picture or the slip of paper she gave me in Minneapolis for some time. I looked feverishly, but it was nowhere to be found. My last remaining connection to the person that changed my life had been lost.

So again, all I want to know is if she forgives me. Now that I know I have Asperger's, it angers me even more because that might have been the contributing factor of my black-and-white thinking on her religious beliefs.

But maybe someday, just like before, I'll get a random message from someone out of the blue asking, *Hi, do you remember me?*

Game Theory

I've noticed that I am a different person when I play a game. Why is that? I have many theories that I'll try to explore to see just what it is about a game that is so liberating.

All my life I have loved games. What did I want for Christmas when I was five? Monopoly. And not only did I get it, I won at it. And trust me, nobody let me win.

I live for the game. As I tell people on Xbox Live, it is not winning or losing that's important, it's the game itself. Through the game I am temporarily free of my mind. Free of Linda, free of Emily, and free of all the other mental anguish. Also, there's no better feeling than the unpredictability of a game set with predictable rules. It's quite hard to explain, I know, but with a game comes so much more than that which is played out.

With my friends in Indianapolis I have probably spent more than two hundred hours playing various games. Scrabble, Monopoly, and Trivial Pursuit are among the vast line of games we have played. And I get shaky just thinking about the pleasure I experience while within a game. In January of 2003, I went to their house and stayed the night. They were all busy, and in the twenty-seven hours I was there, there was just enough time for *one* game of Monopoly. But that one game was quite worth the travel time up and back and the other stagnant hours. One game was so freeing and exhilarating.

Is it the competition of the game? I would say yes and no, because I am impartial to whether I win or lose. The primary thing I want is for a game to go down to the wire. When playing video games, and especially racing games, I will attempt to put the game as close as possible till the very end. I live for the games that are decided at the buzzer. Win or lose, it doesn't matter. I have actually lost many a game trying to make it close.

I'm different when playing a game. The chains that make me not talk and make me overanalyze life are gone. I become so absorbed in the game that all of the rest of the world becomes irrelevant. Also, I am much more talkative in a game. But why is this? What is it about a game that makes me who I think I really am?

In the warm months, I am the chief starter/race director for the St. Louis Karting Association, and at the track I command my post with authority. I have a much better posture about myself, and I move with precision and power. While I take my duties at the track quite seriously, for me it's nothing more than being an emcee of sorts for a game. I'm sort of the game show host for a game that involves people hurling their bodies at breakneck speeds. So, in a nutshell, it's all a game at the track—a game that I am in control of, and I act according to what the rules say.

What the rules say. Those are the key words in this piece so far: the rules. In all games there are rules. And within rules come knowledge of boundaries and limits. For instance, Scrabble can only be played up and sideways, but not backward or diagonally. Monopoly must be moved clockwise, and it's fifty dollars to get out of jail. In a race, there are a set number of laps and many rules governing the way people drive. Within rules comes safety. Within rules comes knowing what's going to happen next, to a certain extent. That's even a more important statement, knowing what is going to happen next.

In the "real" world there are few set rules except laws, and all other rules are determined by the individual. But in a game those elements are tossed out. My overthinking and overcritical attitude toward others is bypassed, because within a game all participants are playing by the same rules. This is Aaron's game theory. I believe my perception of the world differs from yours, but for the short time that a game is being played, the real world and my world coincide, and happiness is found through the medium of the game. So, therefore, winning and losing isn't important because for me it's the joy of that temporary coexistence with others that can't be found anywhere else.

So in summary, within a game everyone is playing by the same rules. When playing a board game and someone disagrees with a play, there is the magical book known as the "rule book." Life doesn't have a written rule book. So how can one who needs everything to have an "official" right or wrong operate in a world that has a gray area of rights and wrongs? Well, it's quite difficult, I can tell you that for sure. But for me, in the short times that I get to play a game, I am free because there are limits and there's a defined beginning and a defined end. In an open conversation, there is no predetermined end to a conversation. So in many instances, I'm thinking, *Is this conversation over, or are they waiting for me to say something?* But within games there are ends. In a race, it's when the predetermined laps come to a close; in Scrabble, it's when the last tile is played or when no words can be played; in Monopoly, it's when I've bankrupted . . . I mean it's when one player remains.

My mom has always asked me why I play so many games, and now I can tell her why. Maybe she'll understand when I can tell her why it was worth thirty-plus hours and five hundred miles of traveling just to play *one* game of Monopoly.

Work

Race weekends were mostly by about waiting. You ran in a heat race, waited a couple of hours, ran in another one, waited a couple of hours, and then ran the feature race. During those couple of hours came the thing I hated most about racing: working on the kart. To touch any part of the kart outside of the driver's area was a guarantee that dirt or grease would get on my hands, and I'm somewhat particular about dirty hands. So I had to be creative in finding a way to get out of that situation.

Enter the eighty-year-old flagman Frankie. Frankie was in the waning years of his flagging career, and it showed. Sometimes a ten-lap race would be eight or fifteen, and sometimes, instead of giving the field the checkered flag, he would give the black flag (which means you've done something wrong and to pull into the pits because you have been disqualified). So my idea was to help him count the laps and hand him the right flag at the right time. Flags weren't greasy. I got my wish in the second half of my first season in 1995.

To be honest, I was after his job from the start. I always wanted to be a flagman of some sorts. And at least now I was the "apprentice" waiting to take over the reins after Frankie retired. During the '95 season I got to do some races by myself when he had to use the restroom. I must say I did quite the job for only being twelve. I can't imagine what adult drivers thought seeing a mere twelve-year-old giving them the checkered flag.

Frankie was forced into retirement in 1997 out of fear he might die in the summer heat. The apprentice was now the head flagman. Even though working for free, I would have paid the club to let me flag. It's the ultimate power rush. The flagman has the power to start the race, end the race, stop the race, and disqualify people. In other words, I was in charge.

My résumé starts at a bowling alley. I had been bowling for one season and wanted to be able to bowl for cheap. I needed money to buy all the good video games that were coming out on the market. So one day at bowling, my dad talked to the manager and instantly I had a job. I would be a lane attendant. Great job: empty ashtrays, bring beer to the bar, and take out the smelly beer bottles.

Before starting that job, I always loved bowling on Monday nights. The reason? The lady who worked the counter the other nights of the week wasn't there and, well, she was somewhat mean and rude to clients. Her name was Carol, and she had *no* tolerance for stupidity or ignorance. The second night I worked, Wednesday, would put me there with Carol. I was just as nervous as I was before my first race. Would she yell at me? I had heard stories that she made other lane attendants cry and walk off the job. So how was she going to treat me?

Right off the bat she was a completely different person from what the legend of Carol was. She showed me everything that Kevin (the Monday-night guy) forgot to show me. She told me that if I got tired I could take a break and that on her nights I could have all the free soda I wanted. This was Carol the Terrible? I was thinking at this point in time, *Okay, when is the nuclear bomb going to go off?*

It didn't the first night working with her, and I was cautious of everything I said. I didn't really say that much, but I was very cautious. Not knowing much about a work environment, I made sure that everything on the checklist was done. I don't know why or how, but Carol the Terrible did not live up to her reputation. Time would not change that.

I started at the bowling alley in September of 1999, while

I was still talking to Linda, and every night was five hours of boredom during which I thought about her. This was the start of the beginning of the end of our relationship. Even though I was very efficient and active in the workplace, there was no escape from thoughts of Linda. Fortunately for me there was a distraction—Carol the Terrible had no problems telling me how stupid other people were.

These moments were bright spots on what was beginning to be a long, dark road. Carol was full of stories about incompetent people she couldn't stand. Maybe she liked me because I wasn't a "phony." I did what she said when she said it and I never made anyone mad, so maybe that's why we got along. While other lane attendants told me about how much they hated her because she was so mean to them, she did something amazing—she got me to talk. Most every night we talked and made fun of the stupidity of certain bowlers. I think she may be the only person who has a more bitter taste for the average person than I do. And maybe it was for that reason that Carol the Terrible was, for me, the best person I have ever worked with.

I got paid only $5.15 an hour, but that didn't matter, because working Wednesday nights was so much fun. I still would dwell on my breakup with Linda, but it was Carol's constant mocking of people that kept me interested in keeping those alleys as clean as possible so I could stay at the counter as long as possible.

Another bright spot was that Carol let me bowl while working. And bowl I did. On one night I played twenty-seven games in less than three hours. And late that summer I would bowl three games that would change my life forever.

On that fateful night, my first game out of the box was a perfect 300. The next game was a 258, and my third game matched my first, 300, for a three game total of 858. I was astonished, and so was everyone else who saw it. (Since this wasn't in a league, I got no awards for it. And still to the day I write this I have not had an official 300 game.) Word got around quickly of the employee who had an 858 while on the clock. The word must have been strong enough for the owner in Florida to hear it.

I missed the following week because I was out of town and I was looking forward to working on Wednesday. I called the alley to let them know that I would be ten minutes late. When the phone was answered, though, it was not Carol but instead Vera, who worked in the snack bar. I asked her if Carol was there and was handed the most devastating thing I could have heard at that point in time: "Carol is no longer with this company."

The person who broke my workplace shyness was gone. But why? The owner liked her and knew that there were a lot of complaints, but he could not get over the fact that she let someone that he was paying bowl on the clock for free. So my great 858 series was instantly nullified because it destroyed my happy workplace.

I started to look for other options. After a brief stint as a film duplicator, which ended with me quitting, I got a job at the video store where I buy games. It was the first job I ever got on my own, not through any connection or help from others. My interview was a disaster, but it proved to be a telling experience for me.

On my first day, the manager told me that I had two weeks to prove that I could make it in the retail world. None of my previous jobs had me selling anything, but here there was so much to sell. For one, we always had to push the "used" games. Also, there were extra warranties on game systems, and then there were also MST, or multiple sales transactions, which were transactions with more than one item. All of these stats were posted in the back room on a big board. And then there was the video game magazine subscriptions and discount card. Little did I know how much this magazine would affect my sales performance.

On my first day, I sold four subscriptions in just a four-hour time span. Was it beginner's luck? How did I convince someone to buy something that I myself had just learned about thirty minutes prior? I was amazed. I was a completely different person when selling that magazine. There was a sense of confidence about me that under normal circumstances was lacking. For someone who was shy and quiet, how was I able to sell something to people? It was amazing.

How amazing? To put it into perspective, the store, on the whole, had three magazine sales for the entire week leading up to the day I started. The manager's experiment seemed to be paying off. He later described the gamble to hire me as: "It was sort of like putting a bet on a horse at a track that has odds of one hundred to one. You know you are going to lose, but yet there's just that slight chance it could pay off." As of now, it was paying off quite nicely.

Maybe what made me so good were all my years of playing Monopoly and convincing people that the deal was good for *them* and not me. Whatever the case, I routinely doubled what everyone else who worked there would sell. When I work, it's a game, but it is a game I cannot lose. *I must win whatever the cost.*

For someone who was as oblivious of other people as I was, I could see eye twitches or a brief glance when I said something, and I knew what path to take to get the sale. Granted, I didn't win all the time, but I always had the highest sales. My career high was ten in a six-hour time span.

Not only was I selling like crazy but I was beginning to somewhat communicate with my coworkers. We were one of the smaller stores, so there was usually just a manager and one employee. This is the element I can talk in. Anytime there was one extra worker, my mouth shut. I simply couldn't talk. One-on-one was fine. Throw one extra person in and it became practically impossible to start or take part in any conversation.

March turned into April, and April would not be forgotten. The store's shrink (amount of merchandise lost/stolen) was always higher than corporate expected. On this one fateful Wednesday, the loss-prevention (LP) guy came in. He interviewed the two other employees, and then he called for me to go to the back room.

He quickly asked me if I knew who he was, and I said

that I remembered him from a time he did a false robbery in the store. He stated that he was from loss prevention and asked if I knew why he was there. I said that the manager always said the shrink was high, so that was why he probably was here. *Trap!* He asked me, "Aaron, do you want to go to jail?"

Jail!? What was this man talking about? Was he insane? Or was this a trick? For the first time I said, "Come again?" Again, there was an awkward moment of silence. It was probably only five seconds, but they were painful ones. What did this guy want with me? Why was he taking me away from selling things people really didn't need? *Oh my goodness,* I thought. *It had to be the Xbox that was out of warranty that management let me trade for a new one.*

Just as I thought that, the guy asked if a certain name sounded familiar. It did. He was a guy who always came in and bought a game just to bring it back an hour later. He had some sort of copying system, and he was bootlegging games.

I told him what that name meant and who was involved. He asked me, "Aaron, why did you not tell me before?"

I responded quite simply with, "You didn't ask." That must have made him mad because he said withholding information could be a sign of collaboration with the crooks. Shortly thereafter he told me to get out of the office.

I escaped the clutches of the menacing loss-prevention guy and returned to work. The assistant manager immediately asked me, "Dude, have you seen a ghost?" He was

saying this because I was pale from the stress of the interrogation.

I didn't realize the ramifications of what I had revealed
to the guy, but I realized that I left out that management
let me have a new Xbox when mine broke. This broke me.
Like a lost child wandering aimlessly, I wandered back to
the clutches to reveal what management had let me do. I
had no idea how severe the punishment was going to be.
An Xbox at the time was still three hundred dollars, and
that could be a severe punishment.

I sat back down in the interrogation chair, and he asked
me, "Why are you back? I told you to leave!" I had interrupted his writing on his laptop. I instantly broke down for
two reasons. For one, I knew my revelations to him were
going to change lives, including mine, but secondly it was
that Xbox. Like the beating heart in "The Tell-Tale Heart,"
there were stacks of Xbox boxes on either side of me where
I sat. I then told him the truth about my Xbox.

Something shocking happened next. He said, "Thank
you." Thank you? Thank you for what? What did I do? Then
he mentioned that the information I provided was vital to
his investigation, and although that Xbox was given to me,
it was the manager who did that and not me. Therefore I
was just the recipient of someone else's wrongdoing. Then
it hit me. Wrongdoing. People were going to pay dearly because of me. It was a repeat of my 858. I had just destroyed
my happy workplace, and this time people were going to
pay dearly. And they might know who blew the whistle. *Oh*

God! My overthinking mind thought of how big the third-party guy was and how he had threatened people if they ever told anyone. I had been told I could be on the receiving end of his threats. *Oh no, oh no, oh no.* Why did this guy make me tell him that was happening? My life, in my mind, was in jeopardy. This made me break down even more.

I had a box-cutter knife in my pocket, and I got it out then. I wasn't going to let the managers or the guy who didn't work for the company hurt me. If I had to, I would get them before they could get me. To say the least, I was a wreck in that small back room. I was stuttering and slurring all my words, and I kept repeating, "I'm a dead man. I'm dead. I'm so dead."

At this point in time, the guy started to talk me down to earth. He mentioned that everything said was confidential and that nothing bad would happen to me, he would make sure of it. I don't know why, but I believed him at the time, and nothing bad did happen to me because I'm writing this today.

I stayed another two months at that store, but every day walking into that back room I was flooded with memories of that fateful April day. Needless to say, a new manager was hired and he must have been aware about the previous situation because he said he would've done the same thing. I quit.

So now I was unemployed again. I had destroyed two happy work environments. Of course, I wasn't 100 percent responsible for the fall of the people who were fired, but I was a contributing factor. I never had worked for the money.

People told me work equals survival. I never could and never have seen it that way. Where I had worked it was always a game. When the game became tedious or the extenuating factors of playing the game became overwhelming, I simply quit playing that game. For me, having no money isn't as bad as working in an uncomfortable environment.

You see, my memory is way too good for its own good, so every time I was in that back room I could remember the tension to such precision that I could sense the adrenaline I felt. I could not remember what the guy looked like, but the chair he sat in was still there, and that chair took on the image of the loss-prevention guy.

I had a few other stints at selling, and a brief one as a bank teller, thanks to my dad knowing a bank manager. The thrill of selling magazine subscriptions wore off, and old memories started creeping in. Soon I became emotionally unable to work.

And here I sit, still unable to. I so dearly want to start a job, but I have trouble starting things. It's not that I don't realize the importance of working for money. For me, though, if it's stressful and emotionally tolling, the lack of money does not outweigh the feeling of hopelessness I feel at a job.

See

I've always liked playing chess. I know all the moves and strategies, but one thing always gets me, and that's my failure to see what the other side does. This is an interesting analogy of how I am in an open social setting. In a chess match—white moves, then black counters. That's how it's supposed to be. For me, however, in both chess and in an open social setting, I am so absorbed in my own move that what the other person does is lost. It's so lost that it becomes irrelevant. I'm so concerned with what I'm going to do that when my opponent moves, I pay no attention to what they have done. Oops.

In a social setting, it's the same thing. However, in Monopoly I can easily calculate moves to win. It's not that I can see what the other person will do, but in that game I can influence what they want by implementing trades, and somehow I know exactly what to do to get exactly what I want. I know there's a difference between chess and Monopoly, but what is it about chess that makes me lose sight of my foe?

I've probably played more than a thousand games of chess, and I am still oblivious to my opponent's moves. People are supposed to learn from their mistakes. For me, however, that does not hold true. Every time, just as in a social situation, I become blind. I do not see. I cannot calculate the other person's variable.

What's truly interesting in calculating outcomes is that I'm great when watching a race on television. Let's take a NASCAR restrictor plate race for instance. Most of the forty-three-car field will be in one big pack. It isn't surprising to have thirty cars on the screen at once. I have a gift and can see trouble before it happens. My mind so quickly calculates what car A and car B are doing that I can see a wreck coming. Ask my dad about this. It must be so aggravating watching a race with me because I'm announcing a wreck before it happens. This is what makes me good behind the wheel. My mind so quickly feels the car and those around me that I can make the right maneuver.

So what's the difference between calculating the movements of cars on a track and another person's chess moves? I'm pretty good at every game I play, but with chess there's this block of blindness that I can't shake.

If I can figure out all of these things in the physical world, why can't I figure out people? Could it be that I'm overanalyzing other people when talking to them? That could be, but I'm not sure if that's completely accurate. I can say it's quite aggravating.

There's no amount of money I wouldn't pay to have my gift of seeing be reversed for just one day. Life is a chess match. There's a move and a countermove. Now, granted, in life people are normally not adversaries, but it's sort of like a dance. One moves, then another follows. With me, as I've said, I move _____ I move. There's a blank where the other person's move is. I try to predict what that blank space is or will be when it's my move, but 99 percent of the time I'm wrong. I grossly miscalculated the way Linda would react to the email I sent her. If I had known that it would have lead to the termination of all contact for what are now five-plus years, I never would have sent it.

That's true for most social predictions I make. I can see perfectly if I'm a third party. If I see two other people talking, I can easily tell what the mood is, if they like each other, and stuff along those lines, but when it comes to the first person, I am blind.

I want to quit being able to see from the position of the third person and start seeing and functioning from the first.

Fear

Fear is an emotion that most people are well afraid of.

As my dad has quoted to me, "As FDR said, 'The only thing we have to fear is fear itself.'" If that's the case, I've got fear of the fear of fear. The anticipation of the fear is enough to throw me in a tizzy.

But what's truly fearful is hopelessness. Can and will things ever get better for me? I can do so many things, but my internal prison is such that I have not found the key. *That is fear*. To realize the problem, to see the problem, but to be powerless to do anything about it is absolute fear.

Fear is what Emily dealt me at the bowling alley with the horrible quote, "You have Asperger's, and no one will like you." Think about that for a moment. I was having a hard enough time accepting myself for having Asperger's, and someone I had known for four years said no one will ever be able to like me because of it. That is cold.

Fear is the absence of the knowledge of what love is. I've

been meaning to use that unknown "L" word many times, and it's been tough to write, let alone think. It's true, though, that I don't know what it is. I think I know about it when it comes to animals, but with people it's like that emotion isn't there. For me love is, "I'd miss you if you were gone." There is no needing that other person's love or approval; there's just my quote. I don't know if the emotion even exists in my head. The closest thing I could compare it to is what I felt for Linda. But not at the time I saw her. I yearn for who she was in Minneapolis and not who she became. Which is it, though—that I loved her in my memory, or that I loved being free?

Does freedom equal love? I wouldn't know the answer to that as I've only been free (meaning being free of my own internal prison) twice. Maybe there's somebody I will meet someday who has the master key to unlock my mind from all its hideous overthinking, but my overthinking mind will overthink so much that just getting into my mind and through all the swirling thoughts is so tough. In both instances where I have felt freedom, it's been a "perfect" scenario.

I do not have fear of the possibility of never being "normal." If I were normal, I might not be able to write the way I do or drive a car with the precision that I do. The fear lies in the possibility that this internal prison I'm in will remain in place.

Now we are coming full circle to "the only thing we have to fear is fear itself." If I allow the fear of the fears to dictate my life, there will never be much of a life. What is so odd is

I have no fear of dying, no fear of hitting a wall while racing, but the fear of speaking to a past friend—and also the fear of not speaking to her—is overwhelming.

— — — — — — —

Loss and fear are one in the same for me. The fear of loss is also the loss of people, which brings fear. A cruel cycle it is.

I'm a person who can instantly become attached to someone or something for no apparent reason. Take, for instance, the legacy of the Minute Maid soda can.

I'm somewhat lazy when it comes to cleaning up if it's outside the "green" zone. The green zone is my gaming area, which has to be in precise order all the time. But back when I lived on Nottingham, my former friend Ryan finished a can of Minute Maid orange soda and put it on the right of my television on my dresser. That can sat there for a month in 1995, and it was still there in 1996. It became part of my room and in some way was a connection with him. That can was there until one day when my mom decided to clean my room while I was out of town. It was gone. This is going to sound pretty odd, but how many people do you know who have shed tears over a soda can?

The loss of that can in the big scheme of things was a small one. People lose things all the time. They might lose their keys or maybe a twenty-dollar bill. But for me it takes only a second of thought and an irrelevant thing becomes important. Even if I still know the person, I can't get rid of it.

I maybe have had a breakthrough dealing with Emily,

but the wound Linda has left has not gotten any better. For me, I have lost her picture, which I promised her I would keep for all time, and now I have nothing. Absolute loss. And I have no one to blame but myself. With Emily it became easy to loathe her, but with Linda, she never did anything quite to the scale Emily did. But I cut Linda off, and now I have nothing to remember her by except her unused screen names and her phone number. Like I've mentioned in prior pieces, I can't remember people. Maybe this is why I become attached to what most would say are irrelevant things. For you, the normal reader, a soda can on a dresser wouldn't endure two days; for me that can endured many years.

Where did this sense of loss start? I remember when I was very young I cried and cried when the space shuttle *Challenger* blew up. I was born in 1983, and I don't recall the year it blew up, but I was young and I realized the ramifications of the events. I knew the shuttle was gone and the brave inhabitants were gone. I, at the time, used *dead*. Maybe that started it.

When I was ten, my two favorite drivers died within months of each other. Alan Kulwicki died in a fiery plane crash outside Bristol, Tennessee, on April 1, 1993. I was an emotional wreck. I know I missed many days of school dealing with that loss.

Several months later my new favorite driver died in a helicopter crash at Talladega in Alabama. Davey Allison would have almost certainly given Jeff Gordon a run for his money on dominance in the '90s, but we will never know.

My two favorite drivers both perished outside of a race car. Since then I have had no favorites. With no favorites, I have minimized the emotional attachment, reducing the risk for pain.

Here's where fear and loss coincide. If I had that much pain over someone I never met, what's going to happen on that horrific day when someone close to me dies? I know I have pain for Missy the dog, but it is so wrapped up in an emotional file in my brain that it's unreachable. She is in what I call a jam.

But if Kulwicki's death was so hard, how will I handle the future? As mentioned before, I have no fear of my own death. With death comes change, and with change comes anxiety, and anxiety fuels pain and then we have a "perfect scenario." This time, though, instead of being positive, we have the ultimate emotional trap—one of which I'm extremely afraid.

There is no avoiding death. Every second that passes is another we lose. Every second that passes is another I know my chances of just knowing if Linda will forgive me diminishes. Every second that passes is another that means you, I, and my animals are reaching our temporal end.

So here's where fear comes in. With every second that passes, I'm stuck here in my internal prison. I so wish I had Emily's external prison. I would much rather be afraid to move about than to be trapped internally by my own mind.

The trapping of my mind is the overthinking. Do I overthink because I simply don't understand what is being said? Interesting question. With a race I can instantly tell you the current situation and tell you where the "big one" is going to happen. But in those terrifying and frequent social situations in which I'm almost a mute, is it that I simply don't know what to do, or that I don't understand what's going on? Very interesting questions; I hope I find the answers.

My birthday is the roughest part of my year. It's another symbolic move toward everyone's fate: The End. My birthday means everyone else is also getting there. Maybe this is where my disdain for change comes from, because maybe somewhere in my mind, if things never change then, well, things stay the same.

I remember as a four-year-old I must have cried for hours when my dad got a new van. Now, why would I care about a change like that? At that age, one's supposed to care about what letter is debuting on *Sesame Street* the next day. So this proves that even from the earliest of ages, I became attached to things rather than people. Do the things that I get attached to represent the people whom I can't remember? Again, interesting theory.

If my memory cannot remember you in physical form, I can remember you through a can, or a letter, or, well, the picture I lost.

Trapped

All of my life, things have remained with me. I dearly wish that I wasn't gifted with such a memory.

With such recall there are so many triggers that can initiate a painful memory. Now, keep in mind, it doesn't have to be a bad memory, because a good memory for me is just as depressing. Every day of my life I walk through a minefield hoping that I don't step on a mine that will make me very sad.

What's different about my memories is that they are sort of "webbed" together. If one mine goes off, the whole field goes up in spectacular fashion. It's sort of like those explosives they use when they implode a building. Once the first goes off, all the others follow.

So what is it that creates an avalanche? It can be something as little as hearing the year 1999 mentioned. Or it could be the mere mention of Baltimore. It even gets so minute that the mention of the PlayStation game *Gran Turismo*

2 can create an avalanche. I got that game December 26 and talked to my then-girlfriend, Linda, on the phone the second I got home with it. The call and the game became intertwined. This is the trap.

I've been told that time heals all wounds, and you have to tell your story a thousand times before you feel better. Neither holds true for me. It's as if the memories in my mind become a vortex that just keeps getting stronger, not letting anything out of its horrible clutches.

So what can I do about this? So far I've found nothing that helps. And if the trend continues, eventually the mention of any given word will start the avalanche.

As I have said before, I don't remember people, but there is no problem remembering rooms, smells, or sounds. I can tell you everything about the lobby of the hotel that I stayed at in Lithuania, but I couldn't tell you one thing about the pastor that we were with. I can tell you that he drove a red VW Golf GTI that had no tachometer. I can easily describe to you what the terminal in the international concourse looks like at the Frankfurt airport, but sadly I can't remember a thing about that pastor. I even saw the tape of the trip yesterday, and yet I can't think of one way to describe him. This is part two of the trap.

Since I cannot remember him, how I remember him is through the memory of the lobby. Maybe I've solved why happy times for me are so sad. Maybe it's because I do not remember the people of the event. Interesting concept, isn't it? The lack of memory creates a vacuum. As I try to remember them, I end up in minefields that remind me of them but not them in form. In other words, I remember "things" about them but not them. (That took enough sentences to explain.) This could be the true trap.

Another almost pathetic land mine for me is St. Elmo, Illinois. What's the big deal about St. Elmo? Well, definitely not its size, as it's a small stop on Interstate 70. But one thing for the longest time set it apart. On the water tower was the town's name, and below it was "1988 I.H.S.A.A. FINAL FOUR." For me this was always a highlight on my many trips back and forth between Indianapolis and St. Louis. For one, going toward Indy I always knew seeing that water tower was one step closer to seeing my friends (see "Game Theory") in Indy. In other words, it sort of became an unofficial gateway. Also, I always wondered about the team that made it to the Final Four. I first saw the water tower in 1993, and it was on there for many years to come.

Then one day, as I was returning from the Brickyard 400, I noticed that the water tower had been repainted. Lost forever for the world to see was the small town's pride that their team had made the Final Four. For me this was a bigger loss. I know it sounds downright stupid. I mean, how could a person associate a town's water tower with so many things? I wish I knew, trust me. But in that instance, one mine exploded into many more. Now every time I pass St. Elmo I remember that water tower's former proclamation. Then my memory will quickly associate that with Emily, and then all the memories with Emily keep backtracking as far back as I can remember. So much pain caused by one water tower. How is that possible?

What else about that water tower? It documented the year, 1988. So in 2001 it was erased. I'm sure that the pictures from the event and banners remain at the high school, but for the outside world it is forgotten. Not with me.

The silly thing about it is that I've never met anyone from that town, and I don't believe that we have ever even stopped for gas in that town, but for some reason the fact that the year was up there on that water tower triggered something in me. It was a reminder of the finality of time.

All my mind's traps revolve around the *T* word. That evil word is *time*. With time comes inevitable change, and change is bad. The removal of the date from that water tower was a symbolic action that demonstrates how time moves on. For me, there is no moving on. I live in a time loop, constantly remembering everything.

I envy that water tower. It moved on. To make an analogy, in my opinion most people's memories are like a train station. People get on a train and move on to the next station. For me, however, I'm still at station one, and my bags have been piling up for many years. I'm still waiting for that train so I can at least drop some of that baggage off at the next stop, but my train has yet to depart.

The true trap is my mind's inability to move on. When my mind can't find a logical answer, the vortex grows even stronger. When I have calculated something in my mind, I think I know the outcome, and if that outcome doesn't happen, a trap forms. I still, to this day, am shocked about the results of that email I sent Linda.

So much of my subconscious thinking is used trying to

find this logic that doesn't exist. Once my mind consciously becomes aware of a logical dilemma that doesn't make sense, an avalanche warning is instantly issued. The really sad thing for me is that it's the same things over and over and over. It's a real *Groundhog Day* (the movie, of course.)

The true mind trap points out that I'm alone (excluding family), but for the most part it's been self-induced to a certain degree. The jam in logic is in the fact that most people don't measure up to my standards (gosh, that sounds overbearing), but I so dearly want someone just to care. So the real trap is the conflict of the two sides fighting back and forth, vying for supremacy. And the two sides are in equilibrium. One side is that people aren't worth knowing (and my memory backs this up), and the other side is the desire to know what that normality on the other side is like. And that now has become the biggest "mine" of them all. It summarizes the past six years perfectly. If the trend continues like I said, will this be the way it is in twenty years? I so dearly, beyond words, hope it isn't. The trap must be broken, or emotionally I will be.

Tomorrow

What is the most fearsome word in the English language? There is nothing worse than *tomorrow*. Tomorrow is uncontrollable. What could happen? Sure, I may get a racing ride and my life will finally begin, but I could wake up to a horror like 9/11. Someone I know may die. Will my animals be okay through the night?

I like and need to know what's going on at all times. While this is truly impossible, I want to be "in the know" at all times. While I'm asleep, nations could fall, stock markets could crash, space monkeys could enslave us all, and who knows what else could happen. That is true fear. During the transition from a today to a tomorrow, one will dream. Dreams are hideously depressing for me. In my dreams I can see people. While awake I can't picture people, but while dreaming those people are remembered in their true form. When I wake up they are gone, and a tomorrow has become a today.

This is what I feel every time I go to sleep. What's going to happen tomorrow? How many people are going to die? Will I know any of them? If someone I know passes, will I be able to remember them? I don't remember my grandma at all. I remember everything about her funeral, but the person herself is nowhere in my mind.

Tomorrow something good may happen, something bad may happen, but no matter how much I wish, tomorrow will come. There are so many things pending in my life that with each tomorrow comes more anger and anticipation. I want to race more than anyone alive. Racing is me. I may not be able to truly connect with people, but when I drive it's like the best dance in the world. The car and I are in harmony. I can feel every movement of the car, and the car does exactly what I want it to do. But with each tomorrow comes one more day that I age. There's a youth movement now, and in an owner's eyes I'm already considered old.

Tomorrow something terrible might happen. There are so many possibilities in the world, and my mind tries to calculate them all. How will I cope if I find my cat dead? What will happen if there's another attack on America? With tomorrow comes the unknown. I am oblivious to any notion that good will come tomorrow. The anger that manifests itself in this thing called tomorrow is indescribable. The rage of not knowing is horrible.

"We'll talk about it later" and "We have to talk" create so much fear in me that I want to keel over and just disappear. If someone says one of those phrases, something must be askew, but what could it be? What have I done? Or what happened?! The anxiety in the unknown is unbearable. And the worst part is that 99.9 percent of everything that happens is unexpected, and 99.9 percent of things don't go according to schedule.

Tomorrow has no timetable of events. It's just a human-appointed time frame of twenty-four set hours. But within those hours, lives can change, nations can fall, and my life could go haywire in a heartbeat. I try to think ahead and predict how it will be, but the monkey wrench can be thrown in at any time.

So the unexpected will happen on any given tomorrow, but on which one? Anticipation swirls around like leaves on a windy autumn afternoon. There is no end. For every time I deal with a tomorrow, another tomorrow awaits. As much as I wish it would, time will not freeze.

While I feel pain of the past, it's fear of the tomorrow that fuels the pains of the past. So in the end, tomorrow will come, but when tomorrow becomes today, there's another tomorrow to deal with. So many unknowns except for the fact that tomorrow I will once again have to deal with the next tomorrow and what joys or horrible pains may come with it. Hopefully, I will be in the know.

Crash

You might think that because I love racing I'd be talking in this chapter about the car-to-wall type of crash. I'm not. The crash I'm talking about is far more devastating. It's the crash of my mind after a day of enjoyment.

It's spring now, and the racing season is starting. I'm still flagging for the local kart club. The first practice was last Sunday. I waited all winter for this day, for on this day I was back in my element. I was in control of all on-track aspects on that day, and I was quite talkative. On these days at the track I am free. Memories are gone, fears are gone, and I can live and focus. Maybe it's because all my mind's resources have to be on the task at hand. It's just like driving a race car. When I'm driving a race car, my mind has to be completely focused on driving. But in both instances, my mind is so focused that I'm in a trancelike state. I can be completely focused and be thinking about the most oddball thing because all my actions become subconscious.

This is the best feeling in the world. On the weekends, I am free. My mind is so focused, nothing else matters. For me nothing else does matter because racing is everything. I enjoy the moments that I drive or flag like no one else enjoys anything else. I am free of all the chains and avalanches and traps and I am alive.

Outside of my element, I am vulnerable to society. In my element, the only thing that matters is the task at hand. In my element, Emily, Linda, fears, anxieties, anger, memories, and bitterness are gone. Then the sun begins to set and the inevitable crash takes place.

There's nothing harder than the final checkered flag of a race day for me. This held true three days ago for the first practice session. As I flagged the last kart and said my good-byes, I walked to my car, and the stressors mentioned above raced into my mind like a dam bursting. This happens every time, and I hate it. Once the crash happens, the mental anguish is multiplied by a factor of ten. I've never known why, though. Why is it that something so wonderful quickly flip-flops faster than the toss of a coin? Shouldn't my time at the track invigorate me for the upcoming week, for there's always next week, isn't there? Logic would say this would be, but it isn't so.

As the final kart crosses the line, it's another symbol that tomorrow is almost here. Another day gone by that I don't have a ride. As much as I like flagging, I don't want to be on that side for my entire life. I want to be the one getting the checkered and not giving the checkered. So maybe, as every weekend goes by and I have my crash, it's because of the feeling that my clock is ticking.

As I start my car and drive away from the track, the crash is normally in full swing. I relive my life every half second. It's such pain I can't breathe or reflect upon the great day I just had. Maybe I crash because I get so mentally exhausted during the day that my defenses against pondering about any given subject are weakened, thus allowing everything to rush on in and get thought about.

The crash, though, is sudden. If it were the stock market, it would be illustrated with a day's trading session, everything going good, and then the line used to show where the market is would just drop off straight down. It's horrible to have what makes me most happy be one of the things I fear the most. I can't wait for this weekend's practice sessions, but I know that there may be another crash come Sunday night.

With tomorrow comes the possibility that I may finally get that phone call and be off somewhere to race. But also with tomorrow comes another day I age. For when I flag or race, that is living; outside of that, what's worth a tomorrow being a tomorrow? Racing is everything. Why does everything else get in the way?

School

My oldest son had severe attention deficit disorder with hyperactivity. Every morning was a disaster. Every teacher's conference was a disaster. Every evening, as he tormented his sister, was a disaster. However, at least he went to school. Getting Aaron to school, now, that was an adventure.

Growing up, there was nothing I hated more than going to school. The anxieties and stressors were always too much for me to handle, but it wasn't always that way.

I remember school wasn't that big of a deal in preschool and kindergarten. I differed from other kids in the sense that I would much rather talk to the teacher about something than talk to the other students. I remember in kindergarten the teacher telling me I would lose my recess if I didn't go play with the other kids. I had no idea why she did that, because we were discussing what math would be like' in future grades and I was learning quite a bit, but then she essentially told me it was wrong to talk to her. This confused me greatly and was the start of my distaste for school.

First grade: The first day of the first grade for me didn't last long. I threw up like I had never thrown up before. Thankfully, I got home in time to see the second half of *The Price Is Right*.

Maybe something else that bothered me was school was now all day long. With that change came a change in the daily routine. It might sound silly, but the fact that the timetable had changed brought about the initial fear.

By no means was I a straight-A student. I didn't care about the grades. I may be somewhat of a perfectionist, but I'd rather play a game at home than study for a test. And in all my years of school, I think I studied less than an hour a month. With my memory all I have to do is hear or read it once and I'll retain it.

I was always ahead of the class in terms of knowledge. About halfway through the first grade I asked my dad what multiplication was. He vaguely explained it to me, but I caught on, and by the next day I had grasped the concept and was starting to multiply.

I felt on top of the world the hour before lunch when I figured out what 7 times 7 was, and I thought the teachers at lunch would be impressed. During lunch I told one of the other teachers that I figured out how to multiply numbers and that I knew what 7 times 7 was. Was she impressed that a student knew how to multiply before he even was doing two-digit subtraction? A big *no* was the answer, and she told me that I wasn't supposed to know that and she revoked my recess for that day. I was crushed. This, too, planted the seed of my hatred of school.

Second grade: I probably had my best teacher in second grade. Mrs. Jendra gave me challenges. When other students would be adding numbers like 10 plus 15 on the chalkboard, I was given problems of 457,292 plus 876,890.

One thing I loved about the second grade was the introduction to geography. We played the states and capitals game. The teacher would flip a flash card that would have either a picture of a state or a picture of a state with a star on it. First one to yell out either the state or the capital would be the winner.

The winner of each round would advance and stand by the desk of another student. When it was my turn, I was unbeatable. There were about twenty-five kids in the class and I won seventy-five matches. Tragically I was cut down in my prime. I was "retired" as champion. The game was played weekly but I was benched. Mrs. Jendra saw my dismay, and I became the game show host: the one who flashed the cards.

Later that year it was multiplication flash cards. Again I was "retired" as champion and became the game show host. But I didn't want to be the emcee; I wanted to be playing the game. This sealed the deal on my dislike of school.

Third grade: The second grade was the start of my poor attendance. The noise level of students talking endlessly drove me up a wall. If I thought the second grade was bad, the third was worse.

The only reason I wanted to go to school was for the games, including multiplication drills. Sadly, the teacher banned me because I would always win. To have the games taken away was nothing short of cruelty. Socializing wasn't my strong suit, nor was participating in class discussions, but when it came to the game, I was a completely different person. Each time, the game was taken away from me. I couldn't understand it.

I missed a lot of school. For the most part it was due to good acting. A thermometer immersed in a cup of coffee while your dad is out of the room works really well.

Finally, after a few more years of bad experiences, extreme noise and chaos, loneliness, our family relocating, and migraine headaches, something good was about to come my way: homeschooling.

There were no annoying idiots in the class (except for my cat), and for once I got to work at my own pace.

By the time I was in eighth grade, I had been seeing a counselor, who had been giving me many tests. I was fifteen, and when the tests were complete I had tested as a sophomore in college. The counselor said it would be criminal to send me to high school. I am so thankful he said that because not only would high school have taken up four years, but socially and mentally I would have been a wreck. His suggestion was that when I turned sixteen to just quit the homeschooling and get my GED. We did that; when I got my test results back, I'd had the third-highest score in the state.

If I had been motivated to be anything besides a race car

driver, I could already be in a graduate school. I did do one semester of college, and I had better results than in my prior experiences, but there was no motivation. In addition, thinking about four years of college sent shivers up my spine. I know, I know, if I had attended college right after I got my GED I'd be done now, but my hatred of school in general persists.

In the end, I don't know what the most stressful thing about school was. It could've been a combination of things. For one thing, there were many times that the teachers said one thing and did another. And then, of course, there's this matter of time.

What pains me the most is realizing how smart I am and knowing what positive things I could do in the world, but this hatred of school will block any major thing that I might want to accomplish outside of racing. My view about the education system is clear-cut; there is no exception. I hate that about myself, but maybe with all the bad experiences and anxieties you, too, would hold school in a very negative light.

Scream

In so many instances in my life the title of this chapter could be used to describe what I want to do. However, since I am not one to raise my voice, the scream is what happens inside my mind. It's not a pleasant feeling at all, so in this piece I will cover the various things that make me scream.

Social settings: To most people I am not what I seem in a public setting. I may appear to be disinterested, self-absorbed, and/or just plain stupid. In many situations, I am only able to muster up one-word answers. This pains me so because I know what I want to say but am unable to verbalize what I am thinking. On the outside I appear to be emotionless, like in a coma, but on the inside I am very conscious of what is going on and the scream is deafening and consumes my thoughts. I know what I want to say, but I am unable to convey it.

So the question is why am I unable to say anything besides a yes or no? On paper it seems rather easy; I know what I want to say, so why not just say it? If it were that easy, I wouldn't be writing this. The pain inside me is so draining.

This is different for me when I'm one-on-one with someone, but throw in one extra element and I shut down. I am a completely different person, and if you're talking to me and someone else joins in you will see me change. On the outside I may look calm, but inside my mind there's a Category 5 hurricane. But why is that? I mean, if I'm talking to someone and one other person joins in, what's the difference? To most people there probably isn't a difference, but for me it's doubling how much I have to think.

You see, in everything I do or say I calculate the various possibilities and the outcomes. If a conversation goes from one to two, that doubles the calculations of what I might say. When I look at the two moments in my life where time stood still, they both were when it was one-on-one. One, of course, was Linda, and the other was with my friend's sister Ashley, who was going to school in Germany and was home on vacation. In both situations the conversation flow was fluent. I had no hesitations, and my calculating mind was turned off. I yearn very deeply to experience that feeling of freedom again.

Freedom is a powerful word. Countries have gone to war and civilians have toppled governments for freedom. I live in a free country, but through my mind I am not free.

It's like being a dog chained to a tree. Sure, with a ten-foot chain the dog is able to travel, but there is no way to go ten feet and one inch. That's how it is with me most of the time. I can experience the ground around the tree I'm chained to, but I do not know what it's like to live without that chain. The chain in this case is my own mind.

So I ask the question: Was it the people in those two instances or was it me who temporarily set me free? Imagine if for your entire life you were unable to feel connected to anyone until for a brief moment, for just a very brief moment, you experienced that. How do you think you would feel? It would be like tasting ice cream for the first time at the age of forty. Then, as you consume the ice cream, it is gone, and there are no refills. That's how it is for me. I know what it feels like, but it can't be duplicated.

The concept of feeling a connection with someone is enough to make me want to scream inside. In addition, what really hurts is that a common feeling for others can be a life-changing moment for me. I'm pretty sure that neither Linda nor Ashley had any idea of the impact they had on me. So here's the jam: Is it them that I miss, or is it simply that for that brief moment in time I felt as if I wasn't alone?

Most of the time I do feel alone. My mind is so wrapped up in thinking about any given topic that it's hard for someone to get through the static. I have only had a real connection with someone twice. This thought leads to an internal scream, because I don't know if something like that will happen again. Both instances were like a tornado. For a tor-

nado to occur there needs to be so many elements to interact to form one. Therefore, I'm the same way, always looking
for the right elements, but all I hear is the scream.

Decision making/starting: I was going to write a chapter
titled "Start," but ironically I had trouble starting it. These
two concepts are two of the toughest things known to
Aaron. Here's an example . . .

I love playing video games, or for that matter games in
general, but video games suffice when there is no one else
to play with. However, there can be a problem before I even
play a video game: deciding which one to play. Call it a jam,
call it a scream, call it what you will, because in the end it's
just downright stupid. What's so stupid, you ask? It's the
lockup I feel when deciding which game to play. How bad
is this lockup? I hate to admit this, but one time I was star-
ing at my pile of games for two hours with no resolution. In
that time span I could have played most of my games for
five minutes, but I wanted to play the right game at the right
time. Think about how many constructive things a person
can do in a two-hour time span. Albeit I wasn't mad at that
time; in fact, it was almost a state of meditation, but looking
back it's so stupid.

We aren't talking about making a decision that could
induce a nuclear holocaust; we are talking about just playing one simple game. The fear for me is that if I have such
a hard time making a decision about starting a game,
how hard will it be for me to make other more important
decisions?

Making decisions has never been my strong suit. Currently, I am the assistant race director and practice day director for the St. Louis Karting Association. On practice days I call all the shots. The club is growing rapidly, and on practice days we split the on-track time among different classes of karts. Last week we had twenty-one rookie/junior karts (rookies are eight- to eleven-year-olds and juniors are twelve to fifteen) lined up on the grid. There's an unspoken rule that on practice days, for safety's sake, there's an on-track maximum of twenty. Now we had twenty-one. Some of the parents came up to ask me what the plan was. This unspoken rule wasn't set in stone. So now I was operating in the most god-awful territory of all . . . the *gray* area.

Racing is all about black and white, or at least who can get there first. Now I had a dilemma on my hands. There are twenty-one karts with an unspoken rule of twenty. All twenty-one have their motors going, and they are all ready to hit the track. The question is, do I split them up, or do I let them all run at once? I was completely frozen considering the pros and cons of each. Then, while considering the options, I felt the saddest scream my mind has ever known. It's one thing to look back on something and think, *Boy, was that stupid*, but it's a completely different thing to realize *at the moment it's happening* just how stupid you really are. I'm supposed to be the director. If I wanted it, the rule could be a maximum of ten, fifteen, or nineteen In my position, I should be able to fire an answer to the parents' inquiries on what the plan is. It took me one long, agonizing minute to finally make my mind up, and I sent all twenty-one karts on track. The next time that group was up I split them, but while operating in the gray area I froze. If the rule were set in stone, I would've had no trouble making the call. That's how life is, though, a bunch of gray areas.

Starting anything is a gray area. Whether it is a conversation or deciding which game to play, it's still all a gray area. On Sundays at the track all the rules are set in stone, or rather a rule book. I operate flawlessly within those rules because I know every option that's at my disposal for penalties and what's legal and what's not. Life doesn't have a rule book, though. Life is much like Saturdays at the track where a split-second decision needs to be made. If you take one minute to make a decision, life can pass you by. There's probably been at least a hundred times that I could've said something or done something that would've made my life a little bit better. But while in the gray zone what should be a split-second decision can take a minute or sometimes two hours.

What happens a lot to me in a social setting of more than two people is a time lapse. It's much like watching a news interview via satellite, but instead of a one-second delay it's more like a couple of hours for me. Take, for instance, what happens to me quite frequently at the bowling alley. There will be a conversation, and I will hear it and start thinking about how to respond, but in the decision-making process all my possible responses are drowned out by my mind's inability to have an instantaneous response because it's trying to think of the outcome. So later I'll come up with the perfect response only to realize that I'm driving home from the bowling alley.

So in essence the "scream" is the self-realization of my shortcomings. I often wonder if my keen sense of self-awareness is a good or bad thing. One thing that causes a huge scream is this self-awareness.

Self-awareness: While writing this piece, I should mention that I'm in Kenya. Three days ago we were in Kibera, a suburb of Nairobi. Now take everything you know about a suburb and throw it out the window. The suburban life of America is nothing like this suburb. This suburb is the mega-slum of Nairobi. The stench is one I will never forget. Trash is piled up on the ground in no particular fashion. While it is the slums, it seemed to have its own economy. For all of the mud huts and houses that would be honored to be called a shack, there were many more vendors. I saw two sellers operating out of the back of the former trailer of a semitruck. So while it may be the slums, the mood wasn't of one of dire straits. Those selling audio equipment had music playing, and when passing by one pub it sounded like a karaoke contest was going on. It was almost surreal. Here is a place where most houses, if you would call them houses, are just one room with no electricity, and people are doing karaoke. There were kids in the streets, obviously hungry, and some even wielding machetes, yet there were people smiling. Even the kids who appeared to be the most hungry politely asked, "How are you?" as we passed them. In the air was a sense of happiness and a sense of pride.

I could not figure this out. To tell you the truth, I was scared senseless and quite confused. It almost depressed me. The depression came because these people looked to be happier than I was.

Don't get me wrong or think I'm selfish. I just couldn't fathom how these people had a sense of hope about them, and here I am living in the most affluent country in the world and I am not happy. Talk about an inner scream. I feel like I am chained to the wall of a prison, my mind, and I am missing out on the world. But there have been instances where I am free, so I know what it feels like. For a majority of people in the slums, the slum life is all they know, and they cannot miss something they do not know. So if the slums are all they know, how could they miss what they have never experienced? They can't, and that's how they get by. If the average American was thrown onto the streets of this "suburb" and lived as they did, he or she would be consumed within a week, if not sooner. So the point is one cannot miss something they do not know. In my keen sense of myself, I unfortunately do realize my shortcomings. And unlike the children barely getting by on the streets of Kibera, I do not feel hope. And just that fact makes me scream.

As with the paragraph above, one can't miss what they don't know. For all the grief that Linda has caused me, I could've been content with Emily even though she drove me crazy. That would be okay if I didn't know there was something better.

So maybe in the long run, as much grief as those two experiences have caused me, maybe they are preparing me for something. Maybe that's true, but I hope that when that happens I don't think of the right thing to say while driving home an hour later.

Kenya

A few years ago I went with my father to Africa, where he was going to do some film work, and I would assist by taking photographs. My dad had been there before. His first visit was when I was eighteen months old. He had had plenty of escapades and adventures. I always thought it would be great to go on one of these great escapades. In the end, I got more than I bargained for.

What's interesting about the ordeal is that when I recall my trip to Kenya, what pains me the most is, of all things, the airport in Amsterdam.

It was about six thirty in the morning when we stepped off the plane and walked into the Amsterdam Schiphol airport after our transatlantic flight from the States. The international terminal of the airport is much like a potpourri of world culture. People from all walks of life rush through the concourse, the shops are in pristine order, and there's always some announcement being made, including many about tardy passengers. Constantly heard were announcements like "Would John Doe flying on Flight 99 to Istanbul please report to the gate. You are holding up the flight. Your luggage will be off-loaded." The accent of the announcer was so sharp that it made Anne Robinson, former host of *The Weakest Link*, seem like a nice second-grade teacher.

The trip from Amsterdam to Nairobi seemed to last forever. I was so tired when we landed that the only thing I could think of was getting to sleep. Lost in my tiredness was the fact that I was in Africa. The luggage seemed to take ages to arrive, but finally we were outside in the fresh air, or rather the fresh air heavily polluted with diesel fumes. Nevertheless, the hotel was just fifteen minutes away.

As we pulled up to the Norfolk Hotel, I was flabbergasted. This place was immaculate in every sense. When we opened the door to our room, there wasn't a word we could utter that described what we were looking at. It was a room fit for royalty. It had two levels and was very spacious, with a bathtub like no other and the best bed I have ever felt. It would be worth anyone's troubles to travel there just to sleep in that bed because sleeping in it was like being in heaven.

Two days later we flew to the town of Kisumu on the shores of Lake Victoria. The first day out, we drove fifty miles or so to photograph some camels. It was a most interesting drive, ranging from what looked like Kansas to what looked like the rolling hills of Kentucky, then to the rocky mesas of Utah and then, finally, to the bareness of the Nevada desert. I never thought I would touch a live, wild camel, but that thought was put away as I got up close and personal with one.

The next morning we set out on the drive that would change my life, or rather how I perceive life.

One of the stories my dad was there to film was the huge number of homeless kids in the lake city of Kisumu—all AIDS orphans. One afternoon as we were driving down a street shooting video, a group of kids spotted the camera and rushed toward us. Within seconds, the car was surrounded and we could not move. It started calmly, but as the driver tried slowly to get away, the tension escalated. Five minutes after we were first spotted, there were fifty to seventy-five kids, ages eight to eighteen, around the car. They were trying to get into the windows and doors and drag us out. There were kids on the hood, the roof, and the trunk. There were kids reaching in and even one kid in the car. Several of them had put their knees below the front bumper to impede our chance of escape.

This went on for twenty minutes while the driver, who knew the area, talked patiently and waited for an opening so that we could make a break for it. As we did so, the kids threw anything they could find, and one of the big rocks destroyed a taillight, not far from where I was sitting in the backseat. If it weren't for our coolheaded driver, we might have been killed.

As we pulled away, I had a shaking in my body that

words can't describe. I remember rounding a corner in the car, then another, then another, then finally we were safe, and my mind went blank until we were back at the hotel. I survived, but the fear and shock I felt that day are still in me somewhere and have yet to be felt again.

In life we all strive for control. Control over money, control over health, control over relationships, control over anything and everything. When control is lost, chaos reigns. And in this episode, chaos ran rampant. I was so terrified that I didn't even know I was terrified. The only word that comes to mind is shock.

Pure fury and pure dismay were what I felt afterward. It was one thing to have nearly had the chance to be in the seats where the wheel of an Indy car had landed, and it's another thing to nearly be killed by a tornado. But this episode was the result of other human beings, and that bothered me. I had never had a firsthand experience of absolute desperation, and now I had an account that will haunt me forever.

That night we got on a plane, and you could have told me that the plane had an 80 percent chance of going down and I still would have boarded it.

We got back to Nairobi. We ended up in the same room at the Norfolk Hotel. It was a healing moment, a place of safety. We didn't do much the next day, and that night we got back on a plane and headed for Amsterdam, and then finally, *finally* home.

It was late afternoon, and when we got back to St. Louis,

the sun was just going down. This was fitting because I, too, was headed down for a lot of sleep. Besides being exhausted, emotionally speaking I lost a lot of myself on that trip. Little did I know it then, but time would reveal the wounds I had incurred in my ordeal.

Desire

What is desire? If given the choice between a relationship and a racing career, a racing career would win out without a second thought. But as of now there is no career, just emptiness. So what do I want? There's only one thing that comes to my mind: understanding. I want people to know the pain I feel. I want people to experience just once what I go through. Sadly, I have no one I know to do this with. I don't even know how many people will read this, but I wish a multitude would so maybe, just maybe, I would feel like someone knows and won't look down on me for me being myself.

Is it too much for someone with my luck to ask for just one experience where I am free? I would give almost anything to have some random person read all my writings, and even if it were just for a millisecond, I'd give the world if they could have just a spilt-second thought of what my world is like. My world is not much different, but this world is much like a space shuttle. The space shuttle has more than one million parts, and if just one part malfunctions, it can cause a catastrophe that cannot be corrected. The space shuttle has one million or so parts, but the world has six billion parts (parts being people), and within each part is a story, a life, and probably ten million internal parts. I'm good with math, but six billion times ten million is a number I don't want to type out. This is my life, and I yearn for it to be different, even just for one day.

There have been a few experiences when the world and I have existed in harmony, but just five days out of twenty-two years isn't much. The thing about it is that a relationship can't be forced, can't be induced, and, in my case, can't be initiated. For something to happen it's almost like a tornado—that is, conditions have to be favorable for something to happen.

All I want is someone to care, to know, to understand. And maybe, for a brief moment, I will be free.

Las Vegas

Two thousand and three had been a rough year. I had a serious knee injury in May, I had my dog put to sleep in June, I hadn't driven a race car in more than a year, and my mom had gone temporarily insane and I had moved to my dad's house. This move took a toll on all my friendships and relationships. The move was sort of like pausing a CD, in the sense that when the move was made all relationships were frozen.

Enter the month of September. My dad had formerly done advertisements for the Derek Daly Driving Academy in Las Vegas. So on a long shot he called and asked if there were any openings for instructors. In a bizarre turn of events, luck was on my side and I was invited to become a guest instructor for a month.

October 4 was upon me, and it was time to start my journey. This was going to be my first solo trip away from home for more than two days without any member of my family.

I would also be staying with a family I had never met. It was truly a journey into the unknown.

The morning of the fourth was an odd one. I got up around four in the morning. Before I left, my stepmom and dad talked to me in the living room. The conversation was one like you would have if you were off to war. I don't remember it because all I could think about was getting on the road. After a lengthy good-bye I was off.

By the time I got about two miles from my house the trip started to sink in, or rather it was sort of like waking up from a nap and having no idea where you're going or why you are even in a car. I quickly called my dad and asked him, "Umm, where am I going again?" Of course I knew the destination, but on how to get there I was blank. He told me, and I quickly regained my bearings and it was to Interstate 70 for what would be the most triumphant drive of my life.

It was 4:50 a.m. as I turned onto I-70 at Wentzville, Missouri. The tank was full and many a mile of road lay ahead. I noticed something on this first leg of my journey: that time flies when it's dark. The sun started to become pronounced as I entered Columbia, Missouri. I had knocked down ninety of sixteen hundred miles. My goal for the day would be to get to at least the Colorado border.

My first fuel stop came past Kansas City right before the turnpike. What was very peculiar was the fact that the three cars I had been following all stopped at this same gas station. I remember that trio of cars well because one was a

Ford Taurus with "U.S. GOVT" license plates, and the person who refilled the tank looked to be a highly decorated airman. It hit me at that point that I would probably never see this person again. I don't know how or why, but instantly, like film, that person and car were exposed onto my mind. I realized that everything I was going to see and drive through I may not pass through again, and then I was reminded of this song that was sung in second grade. I don't remember most of the words or melody, but the final line of each verse was, "Friend, I'll say good-bye because I may not pass this way again."

I had always heard that Kansas was boring, and people don't lie. No offense to anyone in Kansas, but I salute you because to see such dull scenery day in and day out would have to drive you to the brink of insanity.

I refueled somewhere before the Colorado border; by this time it was about two p.m. I was getting a bit weary, but I had to keep going to make it just a one-night drive.

To stay awake, I stopped early for fuel and an energy drink. I bought some shelled sunflower seeds and a Pepsi Wild Cherry. The clerk asked me where I was headed, and I responded that my destination was Vegas and that I had left St. Louis some eleven hours prior. She wished me good luck, and when I walked through the door I knew I'd never be there again. As I entered my car and drove away, what I was actually doing finally hit me; the trigger, of all things, was those sunflower seeds.

Every time I remember my family going to the panhandle of Nebraska, my dad would get shelled seeds. So when I got them, I realized that I was writing my own chapter in my life and that *I* was doing it by myself. It was the first time that I actually felt independent!

At about six o'clock in the evening I finally reached Denver. I thought about driving farther, but thankfully my senses prevailed and I stopped at the AmericInn due north of downtown. This would be my first experience in actually stopping at a hotel and getting a room by myself.

I woke up wide-awake. By the way my body was refreshed, I thought it was eight or nine o'clock. I looked at my cell phone and was shocked that it was just two a.m. I tried but failed to return to sleep, so I packed up and headed to my car to check out and get back on the road.

Within an hour I was in the most scenic part of America I had ever seen, and this was at three a.m. I could tell that the hills on each side of the road were staggeringly high. As I passed each small resort town, the roads became windier and the mountains higher. This was the most exciting road I had ever driven on by far.

All my life I have lived on or near I-70. That interstate runs through my former hometown of Indianapolis and is a main thoroughfare of St. Louis. On numerous occasions we have taken that road east to see my aunt in Washington, D.C. But now, on that day, October 5, I read the sign: I-70 ends. For most people this would just be another transition, but for me it was almost like losing a friend. I had been on I-70 for nearly one thousand miles, and we were almost like old friends, and now it was the end. And when I say end, it's a very abrupt end because if you ignored the exit you would end up in the side of a rock face.

It was about one p.m. Vegas time when finally, finally I completed my 1,660-mile quest. I decided to stop by the office of the academy, which is located at the Las Vegas Motor Speedway. That day there were only two students, and I went with them to the Inner Road Course to observe their class.

As the day concluded, my nerves started to get frazzled as I realized that I was less than an hour from meeting the family with whom I would be staying for three weeks. Anxiety took over. Would these people be freaks? Would they have some sort of strange eating habits or play loud music? The only thing I knew for sure was that the lady's name was Sunshine, her husband's, Freddie, and that Sunshine was a church secretary. Other than that, I knew nothing. Would I have my own room and/or television? There were so many unknowns that would be known in less than an hour.

I drove cautiously and had trouble finding the house, but when I got there, the family was just getting home from work. They introduced themselves, and I instantly felt welcomed. I was shown my room, which had its own television and a fish tank. They had bought bedcovers for me and a pillowcase (which I still use to this day!).

After dinner, Sunshine showed me her cats, and then I went straight to bed, as I wanted to get to the academy early to learn everything I could about what I would be doing. So on Monday, October 6, I was at the track for the first time in a nonstudent role. I was performing the duties of an instructor on that day and all of that week but wasn't being paid for it. It didn't matter, as I was around the cars and was driving a BMW Z3 every once in a while and also serving as flagman, so I didn't care a bit about pay. In fact, to be honest with you, I would have paid them to do what I was doing.

Although the week started out a bit rocky with me being overly guarded and shy, as it went on, I slowly crept into my element. At week's end, another instructor, B.C., went out with me and we drove around in separate Z3s and he helped me learn the optimal lines in a GT car. Then he drove me around, and then rode with me, and it really helped that he was willing to help me out and talk to me. After that, I was right at home at the Derek Daly Driving Academy.

The atmosphere at the house was great. Our sleep schedules were off, so it was as if it was my house. I rarely saw Sunshine, Freddie, or their daughter, Solana. But nagging at me at the same time were thoughts of home.

The day before I officially started working, I went to the Boulder City public golf course to play; this course was class "A" fabulous. If you have ever seen the movie *Casino*, you've seen this course. What was really odd about this round of golf was the fact that I was paired with someone else, and for the first time I didn't mind it. The guy who drove the golf cart was a retired machinist, and I heard all about Boulder City and the surrounding areas and the difference in people from Boulder City and Los Angeles. And do you want to know the weird part about this? It was weird because I actually listened. For once in my life, I cared about some unknown old man's talk. Forever before this, I hated being paired with someone while playing golf because the last thing I wanted to hear was small talk, but now because I was in my element, I actually was enjoying it. It didn't hurt that I started the round with four consecutive birdies.

Later that day, I went to a nearby mall and actually talked to a couple of random people. One person I talked to for about an hour and a half while she worked the Dippin' Dots stand. I asked and learned what there was to do in the surrounding areas but was even more shocked that I, Aaron Likens, was talking to people and actually starting the conversations. My hypothesis was that, for the first time in my life, I was happy. I was happy because I knew that tomorrow, and the next day, and the day after that I was going to go really fast in a race car and that was all that mattered.

October 13 through 17 was a corporate event, and I worked about ten hours each day, arriving at the track at about five a.m. and staying until three p.m. or later. I didn't mind, though, because this was paradise. It was all I ever wanted and more. After each day's work, I would order dinner nearby. Whatever I did, it was the best!

Those days passed, and it was October 23 and I had just one day left scheduled to work, just a half-day school. As celebration of my achievements, Sunshine and her family took me out for a good-bye dinner.

I get down a lot about people, and I often forget the kindness of people like Sunshine.

Once again I went to bed early so I could get up early and work my final day. I wanted to be perfect on this day so I would be called upon again because, as I mentioned before, this was paradise. I mean, I had never had so much energy before. On this trip I felt like a piano player who always played on a small piano that was out of tune, who suddenly got to play on a great cathedral organ for a month.

But, as you should very well know, something weird should be happening soon. I mean, I've written several pages and nothing horrific, terrifying, or bad has happened. I feel some people may read this for the same reason people watch auto racing, and that's waiting for the big one, and my big one was about to happen, but not in the way you're going to think it's going to happen.

As soon as I got to the track, I went to set up the half-day course. I got the cones in place and the cars washed and I was set to go. About forty minutes before the students were set to arrive, I was asked to replace these two ceiling tiles in the classroom. I said no problem, as I didn't want to disappoint anyone, so I went to the classroom to tackle this issue. The ceiling tiles, though, were, of course, on the ceiling, so to get to them, I stood on the table. I managed to get one in right, but the other one wasn't fitting properly. I struggled for about five minutes and then it came down on me. The last thing I wanted was to break it, so I attempted to catch it and in the process I stepped off the table and onto what I thought was the back of a chair I had placed by me. *Big mistake!* I didn't step on the back, but rather the arm, and it flipped over faster than a spinning SUV and I took a head dive.

I don't know exactly what my head hit, but all signs pointed to a Goodyear tire used for demonstrations. I was unconscious for an unknown amount of time until another instructor found me. They instantly called the LVMS crash response team and, before I knew what was going on, I was loaded in an ambulance and headed to some hospital I had never heard of. This was very scary because I was coming in and out of consciousness and I was sixteen hundred miles away from home and no one knew that I was going to the hospital. All in all, it was bad.

Because of the neck injury, I was admitted to the ER and given pain medication right away. I really wish they had mentioned the whole "take with food" catch because I hadn't eaten anything prior to this. Within thirty minutes, I was throwing up. Mind you, I was throwing up while in a cervical collar. I felt so alone.

The doctors prescribed Soma for my pain, and little did I know that I was allergic to it. So, on Sunday, October 26, while heading to church, I lost control of my body movements and slowly turned into a vegetable. This necessitated another trip to the hospital where they gave me some IV medication; within three hours I was back to normal but was told not to take the Soma again (*wow*, who'da thunk that advice?).

By this time I knew I was never going to be an instructor again, and I had no idea what other horrible stuff lay in store for me, so I rested on Monday and told Sunshine I was going to head back to St. Louis the next day. She said I should wait at least a week to let my severe cervical strain and possible slight concussion have more time to heal, but I was so frustrated with the turn of events, I just wanted to be home in my own bed. I knew emotionally I was going to be unable to stand the good-byes, so I had to leave quickly.

So, on that Monday, I went to sleep at four p.m. and woke up at midnight. I woke Freddie, as he told me to, so he could lock the door behind me. As we headed toward the door, he gave me his key-chain thing that has the text and colors of his native Guam. He told me that I was a joy to have around the house and that he and Sunshine would miss me. I held back and simply stated the same thing but in reverse and got in my car and left.

If I had been able to feel emotion at that time, the entire drive probably would've had tears. But I wasn't, and I drove and drove and drove. I made it back to St. Louis with nothing out of the ordinary happening, minus the fact that my neck hurt so bad and that by the time I was home, I could not turn it one way or the other.

I kept in contact with my dad on my way home. He was waiting on the front porch, and as I rounded the corner and pulled onto my street he waved a checkered flag, which was a great symbolic gesture that I had finished my first great journey by myself.

Sadly, though, after that my memory goes rather blank. I do remember driving home from Vegas, recalling those words, "Friend, let me say good-bye, because I may not pass this way again." How true that is.

Film Theory

I have done a lot of thinking since I started writing, and there is one thing that stands out: Everything in life that is major is a "first." Everything that stays with me—whether it be my brief but important relationship with Linda, my eventful trip to Vegas, the *Challenger* exploding, everything—was a first. I'm not haunted by any of the seconds, but just the "firsts." Why is this? Enter what I call my film theory.

Film is an interesting medium. It is a sheet of plastic (polyester, nitrocellulose, or cellulose acetate) coated with an emulsion containing light-sensitive silver halide salts (bonded by gelatin) with variable crystal sizes that determine the sensitivity, contrast, and resolution of the film. When it is exposed to light, it captures a negative image for life and can then be made into a picture of any size. I believe my mind is like film. Once my mind-film captures an image, it can't be changed. It is like a computer that is locked and cannot be reprogrammed. It is, in essence, stuck with that image.

So what if this is true? What if my mind is like a roll of film and every "first" I experience becomes imprinted on this very long roll of film that is life? That could answer a lot of questions, such as the reason painful experiences like breakups and misunderstandings haunt me. Because each was a unique "first," it was captured on film, and remains there, a snapshot captured forever.

This is where I struggle: when a snapshot is captured on my mind-film, it is there for life, and any change of the person, place, or thing it is very hard, if not impossible, to comprehend.

This could be the most important thing I have written about because it could be the key to so many locked doors. I have stated that time is a great mystery and fear to me, and if this film theory were true, then it would mean that my mind is trapped in a different construct of time from other people's. Could this be the reason why there is such difficulty?

Every idiosyncrasy I have could probably be traced back to this concept. Take, for instance, bad language. I remember way back when I was maybe two or three, a bad word was said on a late-night TV show, and my brother repeated it. My dad instantly said that type of language was inappropriate and—*bam!*—a snapshot was taken, and in my mind, foul language was off-limits. Think about that; if every little thing, experienced for the first time, became a frame, can you imagine how long my roll of film is?

There is no chance for a second exposure. Once it's taken, it is done. With that type of mind-set, you can see why life would be scary for me.

The other day I found an interesting and depressing thing. I came to the realization that embedded in the film are other types of memories from the same moment. Call them captions of the time, if you will. Take, for instance, this VHS tape I came across recently.

I love the Winter Olympics. There is no other multiple-day sporting event that has more drama and danger than the winter games. I remember each one like it was yesterday. In 1998, I taped the final day of the Nagano games. CBS had a video recap and then the credits rolled for about fifteen minutes. To most people, this would be nothing, but for me it was an emotional bulldozer that leveled and incapacitated me. How could something so simple be so devastating? Replay the film and add the captions and I believe we have the answer. So much happened during the games and watching that recap made me remember all the events of that February. During the games was the last time I had my friends Paul and Josh over to my house. Dale Earnhardt won his only Daytona 500, and a no-name came out of nowhere to win the gold in figure skating. So many events happened, and in those credits come the captions of the times. When something major or minor happens, it gets on the film: everything in life gets on the roll. To make yet another analogy, imagine a memory on steroids and that's what I'm describing.

What I just realized is that the captions are the triggers that ignite the memories.

The story I'm going to tell next will probably be the most painful and deepest part of me I have ever exposed, but now I understand why it is the way it is.

It has to do with Ashley, the first girl I ever met outside of my family. In late 2003 I was in Indianapolis. On that evening I played a game of Risk. *Oh sure,* you're thinking, *everyone's problem is that darned Risk game.* The people playing were my friends Christopher, Matt, Kim, Ashley, and me. I've known each and every one of them for as far back as I can remember, and I want you to remember this sentence.

Later that evening, their mother, Anna, asked me how my relationship with Emily was going. I stated that things weren't going all that well and that I didn't actually care that much for Emily. Before I could finish the sentence, Ashley told me to get out of it. Ashley was studying in Europe, and this was the first time in five years I had spoken to her. We must have talked about all sorts of different matters for about two to three hours, and I had never felt so free. But why?

It's found in the words "I've known each and every one of them for as far back as I can remember." The answer is right there. If the film theory is true, and I believe it to be, then this family, and Ashley, in particular, was the first family I remember outside my own. Put it all together and you get a first.

Since she was the first girl I ever knew, all others, no matter who, would be compared to her. It didn't matter if I liked Ashley or not, she was the first one I knew. So from four to my current age, she was the "film" for girls. Now, in this instance, on this fateful Christmas of 2003, I was talking to her, and I was completely open. It was so seamless and easy because since the film was already there, I was already in my comfort zone.

When it was time for me to be picked up, it was over, but that snapshot was taken, and today it is sort of like the Pulitzer Prize–winning photo that is shown over and over.

This can be extremely painful, because there is no escape, no respite. Difficult experiences, like breakups and the loss of friendship, are bound up in these memories, seared into these frames of film. And when there is no way to erase or evade them it sure makes the future scary because, if it is true, losing things will be really hard. I haven't lost too many things in my life. The only things I can think of are a grandmother, three houses I lived in, contact with Emily, Linda, and Ashley, and Missy the Maltese. Other than that my experience of loss has been minimal. How will I be able to live thirty years from now?

If my theory is true, it is necessary for every print from the film to be the same. For me to find someone will be difficult because if they don't fit in the framework of previous images (Ashley), compatibility will be quite difficult.

Think about it. What if every small snippet of your childhood was fused onto your brain and the hard drive couldn't be cleaned? Everything you learned that was a rule was added to the list of film and there was no compromise on any of it. The world would truly be a scary place.

I've read that some people with Asperger's aren't diagnosed, like me, until about age sixteen to twenty-two. That makes things difficult. If film theory is correct, normal people are erasing and throwing away old photos while the person with Asperger's is hanging on to a huge scrapbook. This is why there's a dynamic social separation at that age. Maturity comes from moving forward to new images, new frames.

But people like me can't let go of the old footage. According to my film, every friend should be like Matt, every girl would have to be like Ashley, every career I would want would have to be like racing, every time I go anywhere far I have to have a Red Bull, every time the Indy 500 rolls around I must go to a bookstore the day before the race, every time I write a piece, the headline must be in eighteen point. The list could go on and on.

Whatever it may be, I am completely petrified when someone tells me that everything and everyone changes because for me if it isn't like I first knew it to be, it is downright terrifying. So with that said, maybe now others can understand just how scary the world is and how dire it can look from my eyes, because where you see change for the better, I see what was there before, and always will.

The Darkroom

Somewhere in everyone's mind is a darkroom, where film is developed and prints are made. Before the darkroom, the film is just on a roll, but after the transformation, it can be enlarged to any size. So what's the point of this darkroom of the mind? People every day take mental snapshots of their day and a lot of film is simply thrown out. For me, however, my rolls of film have forty-eight exposures compared to the normal twenty-four. As I've mentioned, here's the important part: every one of my exposures stays with me, and the entire context of the photo can be relived in a heartbeat. The photos have to be relived because they are burned into my vision of life.

In "Film Theory," I mentioned that I believe my mind takes a photo of important events, and the photo is then etched in stone. I can remember when I was four and we (my dad and I) drove by a discount store. I wanted candy so

I asked if we could stop. My dad told me no because that store had sticky floors. Now, whether or not they do is immaterial. What is important is on the photo of that sunny day back in 1987 I was told something, and to this day it remains as law.

So this raises a question: Is there a *me*? Have I ever created a photo by myself, or have they all have been influenced by third parties? At this point in time, I can only think of one that I have created on my own: racing. Maybe that's why racing is so powerful and important to me.

What makes the film in my mind such a defining part of my life? Could it be that from an early age I did not have the street knowledge to make sense of life, which was coming at me faster than I could process? If so, did my mind become reliant on these firsts to set the norm forever? Very well could be. Whatever its origin, my darkroom is open twenty-four hours a day, 365 days a year, and it makes for a difficult process of capturing and understanding.

Here's the main problem: if I wasn't exposed to something at an early age, when the majority of film was first exposed, I don't tolerate it. I lost at games when I was young (though not often) so, therefore, it is tolerated, almost like a vaccination. If an experience hasn't already "vaccinated" me at this point, it simply is not tolerated.

What are these pictures in my head? Here are a few that come to mind . . .

- Mediocrity is the end of life. To be mediocre at anything is not acceptable.

- Money is the key to happiness and also the root of all internal fears.

- Winning isn't required. Respect from the competition is the real way to win at a game.

Those are some things that come to mind, but at the same time, throughout my life other photos were taken that aren't as positive and made their way into the film. They include:

- I am completely unlikeable, for reasons unknown.

- Bad things happen to me by the bucketful (this one has been proven true).

- People in general aren't good; evil is everywhere because the rules aren't followed.

I'm much like a mile-long train without brakes, going down an infinite hill. Once the train is moving, there is no stopping it; so, too, with my brain and its photos. And all it takes is one thing, one minor, insignificant thing, to launch a train.

I know one can't live a happy life when one can't see hope. Hope is what makes one get up in the morning. Hope is what sparked revolutions. Hope is the essence of happiness. And for me hope isn't in the dictionary. Maybe I should check the thesaurus.

Maybe . . .

Maybe today will be the day that things are figured out. Maybe something, anything, will happen today. My existence is a hard one, and maybe today will be the day that I lose the painful memories. Or could today be the day that, out of the blue, I receive a phone call that changes my life forever?

There are so many things that could be and need to be. Perhaps today is the day that the world may get a slight glimpse into the life of a person who has Asperger's. Maybe somebody somewhere will have an inkling of a notion on understanding it, and then they may share that with others and maybe, just maybe, over time, the pain and agony will be understood.

But then again, maybe the pain and suffering don't have to be. Maybe I will just become normal. Likely not, but maybe it could happen. Maybe I will learn what life is about today, tomorrow, or this month. What makes the world tick? What does one have to do to know happiness? Maybe today I will find out.

I am stuck in so many maybes that it boggles my mind. Perhaps the maybes will be reduced today. Maybe today is the day that the names of certain people won't send shivers up my spine. Could today be the day that the present becomes the past and the future becomes the now? The present has been so for nearly five years. What will it take to allow the future to come to the present? It's so difficult to be stuck like this, but maybe today will be the day that all that will change.

This is the world I live in. Like a car on the side of a highway with a flat, I'm not going anywhere, fast. The only things I have right now are the maybes. A maybe has never been a safe bet, and it is not a fun world to live in. Every day I hope that just one maybe will become true. I wake up every day hoping, wishing, that maybe that phone call or email will come. Sadly for me, I go to sleep every night with the same wish I had the night before.

What is even more aggravating is knowing that so few people have a clue about why I am the way I am. When people ask certain questions like, "Do you have a job?" or "Do you work?" and I say no to both and then they look perplexed, I know that the next question is, "Well, what do you do?" To explain what I have is like trying to sell an ice cream machine in northern Alaska. In other words, they look at me like I'm speaking French and they speak Japanese.

So as the sun is four hours from breaking, maybe today will be the day that my life will start again. Maybe today is the day . . .

What Does It Mean . . .

. . . *To survive?* This is a tricky question to which I don't know the complete answer. Emotionally speaking, survival is possible when the stressors around me are at a minimum. Money issues, for example. To work to earn money little by little is way too stressful for me, worse than the stress of having no money at all. It's sort of like a "go big or go home" attitude. That mode of thought is very discouraging because I realize my shortcomings.

- - - - - - -

. . . *To love?* My mom once asked me if I loved. She was speaking in general terms, but other times she has asked if I loved her. Before her question, I had never thought about the actual emotion of love. It was always a reflexive response: if person A says it, person B should respond with the same.

As I thought about my answer, I instantly became jammed. Five minutes passed. Ten minutes passed. As the minutes ticked away, as painfully slow as a bad infomercial, I could not think of anything to say. Finally, I came up with the line, "I'd miss you if you were gone." That was it. This is all I know about love. There is nothing deeper. Maybe when it comes to love, that's as good as it gets. I don't really know, though.

I can't put into words the deep sorrow this gives me. To see others who appear to be in love and knowing that quite possibly the deepest emotion of love I will ever feel is of an "I'd miss you if you were gone" variety is so, so painful.

- - - - - - -

. . . *To be happy?* Happiness for me is when I am completely disassociated from the world. I get this feeling when I'm driving a race car. While driving, like I've mentioned now what must be a thousand times, it's just me and the car as one. Relationships don't matter, living doesn't matter, and the only thing that matters is going one-tenth of a second faster. I do think about the rest of the world while driving, though. It's the only time it makes sense.

Happiness is also days that I flag a race. It is also sad to think about those days because it could be used as an analogy of Asperger's. Just as in a normal social situation, I am isolated. Most contact comes via the radios, as opposed to immediate personal contact. The key thing is that I am alone, yet functioning. What I do when flagging I do to the best of my ability, just like everything else I do—and just like everything else, it doesn't involve other people. So while flagging is one of my happier times, it is still a stark reminder of the bigger picture, because the two are very similar.

Happiness comes in memories, which in turn cause sadness. My memories get turned around. Most times of my life that were generally bad get turned around in the present and are made to look like they were really good. It is so very hard to know what happiness is in the present when happiness in memories is overwhelming and, in fact, happiness in my memories wasn't really happiness at the time of the memory. So how can one be happy when one doesn't even know what it is?

To live, one must have a purpose and a reason. To drift from day to day, month to month, and year to year with no destination is not conducive to a happy state of being. Unlike others who drift their entire lives, I know what I want. But right now I'm not doing what I want, which gives me a driftwood-like appearance. This is most aggravating, because I am not like that.

When people ask me what I do, and why I'm not in school, I have no answer that they will understand. The general public would better understand thermodynamics than the ways of someone with Asperger's. To have people assume *Well, maybe he's lazy* or *Maybe he's retarded* is so aggravating that it makes my arteries pulse with rage. There is no happiness here, and it happens day in and day out.

If I were told I had the chance to never leave the house again and that all food and services would be provided for me in my house, I would not hesitate for a second to accept that offer.

- - - - -

. . . *To be good?* To be good means to be the best. If you try something, you should try to give it everything you've got. The ultimate goal in anything, in my opinion, is to be nothing short of number one. For me, if I can't be better than average, then there is no reason to do it.

This mode of thought clashes with the general public, though. My mind-set is the same in the workplace, and therefore I hate slackers. In every normal job I've had, eventually I get to the realization that no matter how good I am, it doesn't matter. Being the fastest at the bank won't help me find happiness. Selling a horde of magazines at the video game store won't help me get more of anything. In every workplace, I was typically overall the best performer, but what's it worth? Why be good? Why try like heck to sell the magazines when there is nothing in it for me? I would make the same if I just sat around and barely did enough to keep the job.

Those questions make me go temporarily crazy. I must be the best, but why do I try so hard when it gets me nothing? One could argue that knowing I'm the best would be enough. I would make the counterpoint that unless it is shown or stated that I am the best, then I don't know it.

Unless it's big, then it isn't worth doing. Why be normal? Why conform to the status quo of society? If one is good, shouldn't they be rewarded for it?

— — — — —

. . . *To be friends?* A very painful question indeed, because I do not know what a "friend" is; nor do I know how to make them, what to do when the rank of "friend" is achieved, nor do I know who calls me friend.

- - - - - -

... *To be alone?* This is much like a coin, as it has two sides. On one side, I love it. There is no conflict (besides the self-conflict), there are no added stressors, there is no worrying what the other person is thinking, and there is no need to be concerned about anything about anyone else.

However, I have known what it is like to not be alone. Life is more interesting with others. One would be unable to climb Mount Everest without a team. One would be unable to do much of anything without others. So is there no happy medium? Well, there isn't. This is very paradoxical. And living within a paradox is very confusing, to say the least.

If others typically only let me down, then why know others? But would life not be mundane without others?

Others are unpredictable, but the predictability of being alone is so predictable that it is downright painful. The point/counterpoint could go on forever, and for me the two are in equilibrium. I am living in an ambivalent world. Not fun in the least.

- - - - - -

... *To be the best at any given thing?* This is sort of like the question about being good, but this question is about when the facts are clear that I *am* the best. I do have a very simple and very sad answer when I know I am the best ... There's just emptiness. There's nothing. There's more substance in a book of blank pages than there is joy in my head when I know I am the best. When I got the number one score over-all in *Forza Motorsport* (an Xbox racing game), the jubilation I felt was nonexistent.

So why do I strive to be the best, since when it is achieved I feel nothing? It's much like a dog chasing its tail. While the dog has the goal to catch the tail, it won't know what to do with it once it succeeds. Very much like me. I chase and work and struggle to get to be the best, but when I get there, I don't know how or what to feel. The only thing I feel is something along the lines of, *Well, that's where I should be.* The emotion of joy simply doesn't exist for me.

— — — — — —

. . . To know or want something and be unable to do anything about it? This question is like a huge umbrella that covers a lot of topics, but the answer for the most part will be the same.

To know what I want and to see it pass me by is much like watching a train going down the tracks and seeing a car in the distance parked on the tracks. The only thing you'd be able to do is watch helplessly as the speeding train obliterates the parked car and any occupants. This happens to me every day, except in my case, I am in the parked car. Day in and day out I get hit by many speeding trains; trains symbolize many different things.

What things? There are many. One is just the art of talk-ing to others. To want to talk and to be powerless is much like stalling on the tracks. To want to talk to someone in particular and to be powerless is the most helpless, saddening feeling in the world. It's not that I don't want to talk to others (believe me, I really want to!), but it could be just as blind people wishing to see . . . They're unable.

– – – – – – –

. . . *To be comfortable?* The first answer, as predictable as it may be, is to be in a race car. Outside of that, there aren't many. Well, outside the walls of my home there are none. I'll probably never be at my friend's house in Indianapolis because now he's married. I may be there at some point, but it certainly will never be the same. I have worried about the coming of that day since I was about ten and until now have felt nothing about it. Basically my only other place of comfort is somewhat gone now. And the thing is, they probably don't even know what they have meant to me.

I have so many memories with that family and, as I have written before, I don't remember people in my memories. Why is this relevant? I can only recognize someone if I see them in person. Once I recognize them, I remember everything that happened when I first saw them; for instance, three days ago I saw a police officer shooting a radar gun on a road. It's a rather slow road, so I was able to see him, and instantaneously I recalled that this same officer had been shooting radar about a mile down the road . . . six months earlier. He had been shooting radar when I was ordering at Steak 'n Shake and I was about a week or so from going to Africa.

Why is this relevant? Because things will never be the same in Indy, and for all I know I will only have memories, and without seeing them in person my memories will just include me and only blurred images of them. If I see a person, they get inserted perfectly into my memories, but ten minutes later they're a blur again.

——————

. . . *To be me?* One word: painful!

Small Things

I operate on the big level. If it isn't something out of the ordinary or a five-hundred-foot home run, I'm typically not interested. This makes for an interesting contrast to the importance of irrelevant things.

As I think I have written earlier, there used to be a soda can on my dresser. It was there for more than three years, and then when my mom cleaned my room it was gone. The level of sadness felt over the loss of that can was ridiculous, but even so the question has to be asked: Why is there so much sadness over a can?

There are so many things right now that I am keeping that could be compared to that can. The number is staggering. What would be just a piece of trash or an irrelevant instruction booklet from a game made sixteen years ago would be something I could not part with. Every little thing has a memory. Every little thing I keep, I keep because I can remember every small detail about it.

There's an interesting contrast here, in my opinion. I'm the type of person who, if given the chance, would travel the world years on end. But at the same time, I can't bear to get rid of an instruction booklet from a game I don't even own anymore or throw out a controller that doesn't work.

I haven't figured out how long something has to be in a certain locale before it obtains the status of "immovable" but, in any case, it shouldn't be there. How can one feel sadness over a can? To tell you the truth, I think I can honestly say I felt more lingering sadness over that can than I have for Missy, my dog who passed away. How can that be?

Here's my theory: That can represented more than the Minute Maid orange drink that was in it. The year it was originally placed on my dresser was 1998. The soda can was placed there while Ryan was over and we had just conquered *Final Fantasy 3*. The next week, I went to North Carolina, and when I got back, just like my house, the can was still there. The can was there when I returned from Minneapolis and sat there, as it always had, looming with a hint of vagueness. It was there but not prominently.

The can was there as I went to Alaska in 2000, and when I returned, the can was still there to greet me. The can was there the day I first met Emily; then tragically, a week later, the can that had sort of been a staple in my life was gone. Thrown out like a normal piece of trash. It was treated just like these four cans to my right as I write this will be. Discarded and/or recycled.

I know it sounds silly, but that can really meant something to me. There are, as I have mentioned, other things that have a similar meaning to that can. One thing that pops in my head is the defunct air freshener I have in my car.

I bought this bear-shaped car freshener in Las Vegas just to buy something at a store in the mall in Las Vegas as a means to talk to someone. This was bought back in late 2003, and its air-freshening capabilities have long since passed, but there's no way you could get me to throw it out. That car freshener was with me my entire time out there after I bought it. It was with me all the way to Florida, D.C., and countless trips to Indianapolis. It was with me on a number of dates with Emily and what would be the last date I would have with her.

Such simple things to you are items of monumental proportion to me. And what is so aggravating and irking is that I realize the near stupidity of it all, but it's like trying to reprogram a computer virus when you know nothing about computers. In other words, it's impossible for me not to get attached to small items. But what's weird is that I don't get attached to semi-relevant items like keepsakes or collectors' items. Yup, why spend fifty dollars to get attached to something when all you need to do is drink a soda, place it on your dresser, and enjoy!

There are other small things that I don't get to enjoy that don't relate to cans or bears. The small things are simple conversations. Outside my family there are minimal occurrences when a conversation takes place. Sure, I talk at the racetrack, but for the most part I'm either giving orders or answering yes-or-no questions. In other words, everything is skin-deep. It's been one and a half years since I had a conversation outside this house like what normal people experience on a normal day, a conversation that is just that, a conversation. Unscripted, unrehearsed, and unplanned is what this conversation was.

Normally, I am prepared in every conversation for every possible response. It is sort of like being a defensive coordinator for an NFL team and having to know every play of the opposing offense. Such is how I am in a conversation. When for most people a conversation flows like a river, I am guarded and play the conversation much like a chess match. A chess match, you ask? In chess, black starts by countering white's moves, and the number one goal is not to get trapped early in the game. That is my conversational goal, normally. I just give a simple response so I don't get trapped in an area that I don't know or don't want to talk about. But on this night that I have mentioned before, all the rules I live by were thrown out.

On paper, a conversation between two people is a common occurrence that doesn't require much fanfare or someone writing about it five times. (Can you tell I am stalling in mentioning what exactly this conversation is?) On this fateful Christmas night of 2003, I would experience a taste of normality. What is a small thing for the common person I got to experience for just the second time in my entire life. That's not to say that I have never talked before, but this conversation wasn't played like a chess match. Much like the can, though, what is significant for me is just another thing for the other person. What was the only shining spot of the second half of 2003 (minus Las Vegas) for me was probably just another day for her.

Looking back, I don't know if I would have wanted to have that conversation. That two-hour talking session then was great, but now, since there's nothing, there's only the knowledge of what I am missing. That brings up the question, "Is it better to have experienced something once than never experience it at all?" Right now, I can easily answer that question by saying I wish I didn't know, because one can't miss something they are oblivious to.

I can justify my yearning for that conversation by saying that was one of my few tastes of normality, but what about the irrelevant items? I still am at a loss for words when it comes to defending how I can miss a light piece of decorated aluminum.

Anyone who has ever moved anything of mine can say that I get a bit testy when I find it moved. Take, for instance, race days when I flag. We have the start line about eighty yards toward turn one, so the speeds are lower in the interest of safety. If there is someone on the straight to help slow them down, they will normally grab a flag out of my holder to signal to the drivers to slow down. But when they go to put back the flag in the holder, they *never* put it in the right spot. They will always put it in the wrong holder. You see, I have a scientific process in the way I have my flags, but I always have to rearrange back to perfection when someone tampers with it. This, too, is how my rooms are at home.

While they look like a mess and look like everything was thrown together haphazardly, everything, in my eye, is in its proper place. While there's a pile of wires and controllers, I know where everything is and what the order of it all is—that is, until someone moves it slightly. Or there's always the dreaded "cleaning day." Nothing's worse than cleaning day, because if I'm not around for it, I never know if I'm going to lose something like that old can.

For me, it will always be on my dresser, always there rain or shine, sitting there as it has been since day one.

A Friend Gone

Recently, I lost a close friend. This is important because I don't have many friends and, like me, she was quite shy. We shared many traits like that, but she's gone now.

We were friends for more than thirteen years. She was always there for me when I needed her and sometimes when I didn't need her. She somewhat shadowed me. I didn't mind this, though, as like I said, I don't have many friends. But the friends I have are close and very important to me.

Her name was Amsterdam. That is a very odd name unless you are a cat, and then any name goes. Yes, this close friend was a cat, and what a wonderful cat she was.

Much like twenty-six months ago with Missy the Maltese, I had to make the decision to have her put to sleep. I can't think of a more difficult choice to inflict upon someone. I knew her from when she was less than three weeks old. I bottle-fed her when she was just larger than a softball, but now instead of nourishing life, I had to make the choice to end it.

Amsterdam was always there for me. At first, she was excessively shy around everyone, including me. Then one night, she was walking around with a piece of dog food in her mouth. She wasn't eating it but just carrying it. She dropped it by me, and I threw it toward the front door and, like a dog, she went after it and grasped it with her mouth and brought it back. We repeated this throw-and-retrieve game at least a dozen times, and after that we were best friends until the end.

She was there for me when it was Missy's time. In a way, she took Missy's spot on my bed, and she became very dog-like in her loyalty toward me. I guess it's sort of ironic that the same ailment that took Missy away would claim Amsterdam.

Shortly after Missy was gone, Amsterdam began losing weight, so we took her to the vet. The vet did a blood test, and it came back with all the signs of kidney failure. The vet gave her at the most six months to live. That was twenty-six months ago.

I don't know what drove her, but she didn't go quietly and did not succumb to the all-but-terminal news. It was like she didn't get the memo that she had six months, because shortly thereafter she put on the weight she had lost, her gums regained their color, and she got her youthful step once again.

I think she could feel the deep loss I had over Missy, and she wasn't going to put me through that again so soon.

Time went on and I forgot about the grim diagnosis that the vet had given.

Every morning when I got up, Amsterdam would be on my stomach, at the foot of the bed, or on my dresser that lies about two feet from my bed. I have had a lot of health stumbles myself this year, and the past month I didn't realize that she was no longer by me when I got up. Instead of being near me, she was either under the television or in the front room's main window. I also did not realize the weight she was once again losing.

Then, just a week and a half ago, while I was about to go to sleep, I was eating some string cheese. This is my other cat's favorite food in the world, and Amsterdam didn't mind it, either. On this night I gave a piece to Amsterdam, and she started to eat it and then spat it out. I was about to give it to Siam when I saw what appeared to be blood on it. I assumed that it was probably a tooth or something else that would just go away.

The next week she didn't move about the house much, and I was still oblivious to her declining health (I had a concussion this same month, so I was a bit slow). Then one morning, Siam started to be extra talkative for no apparent reason. He is a very talkative cat, but his tone and sense of urgency were different. I called for Amsterdam and got no response.

She was very loyal and would always come when her name was called. I panicked and went flying through the house trying to find her. I went down into the basement and called for her again and there was nothing. As I got back upstairs, I heard what sounded like the mail slot opening, so I went to check the mail, but there was none. As I turned from the front door I heard this faint meow, or an attempted meow. The past two weeks she hadn't made much noise.

I looked at her and realized she had this shiny substance under her mouth. I walked toward the kitchen and kept calling for her, and she followed quite willingly. As we made it to the kitchen, I picked her up and then it was made clear. It wasn't a hairball, or thrown-up food, but instead was the crimson color of blood. She was dying.

I knew immediately what choice I would have to make on that day. The choice was clear, but the timing was so sudden. I had not had the mental capacity that month to realize she was on her way out. So for me this turn of events was quite sudden.

I called my dad, and he came home and then I spent my last moments with what was one of my last remaining friends. I sat her on a chair adjacent to mine and I just petted her and talked to her, and she just sat there as if she knew what was going to happen and she showed no fear. While her body was going through its last stanza, she purred while I held her.

With what would be the last time I would hold this dear cat, I held her over my head and I just looked at her. All her life, she would just keep eye contact for a brief moment, but this time she just stared at me to the point that it appeared like she was looking straight into my soul. The way she was looking at me was with a sense of contentment and fulfillment. It was almost as if she was speaking straight to me through her eyes, saying, "Aaron, it's time. Thank you for taking good care of me. This isn't the end, as I will see you again."

Whether she really was saying that or just going senile as her body was failing, I will never fully know. I can say that in thirteen years she had never looked at me like that, and I know it wasn't a look of pain.

After she pierced my soul with her eyes, it was time to hand her off to the car ride that would be much like a condemned prisoner taking his last walk. As I handed her to my dad, I kissed her head and I told her, "Thank you for being such a wonderful cat," and then she did something she had not been able to do for two weeks. She meowed. And then she was gone.

Mary, my stepmother, told me that while she walked into the humane society holding the box that Amsterdam was in, she talked to the cat, telling her that she was just about to arrive in kitty heaven. Then for what I think would be the first time ever, she meowed to Mary. Amsterdam kept to herself and never really liked Mary. In fact, she pretty much just liked me and barely tolerated everyone else. I guess from her viewpoint, everyone else was just a distraction and a barrier that could get between her and me. I never had thought about it, but after the soul-piercing look and her response to Mary's comment, I am sure that pets are much smarter than they show and that each of them has a soul.

Mary had to take her because I knew that I would not have had the inner strength. From the time they left with her to the time they got back, I worried so much that she might have panicked. I hated myself for this. But then I remembered that look of contentment she gave me, and it was almost a preemptive look of forgiveness.

She had never looked at me like that before, and I am fairly confident that what I thought she was telling me is true. So, my dear Amsterdam, I once again thank you, and I know it isn't the end, and someday I hope I get to see you again so I can apologize for not being able to take you myself.

| . . . |

I wonder about a lot of things, but most of all I wonder what exactly I am. The first logical answer that comes to mind is a bunch of water, but beyond that, what exactly makes me tick? The dumber version of that question is "Who am I?" I know exactly what I am, but knowing that makes me ask the question because it is so paradoxical. Since no one can fully know who they are, one who does doesn't really know. The illusion is what they think they are. This is what Asperger's is! With all the firsts and rules, it is very clear what I am and who I am, but in real society that simply doesn't work.

As confusing as that first paragraph was, I assure you that it is all the more confusing for me. The summary of that paragraph can be compared to the phrase, "One who thinks they know it all knows nothing." I believe this is the self-awareness aspect of Asperger's. If someone is so keen on knowing everything about them, it creates a slew of issues.

One thing is a closed line of communications because they may think, *I know who I am, and you're wrong, end of story!* Another example may be that they don't want to communicate any emotion, because since they know it all too well, it is just overwhelming. And lastly, they may come full circle and get to the part of knowing nothing and be so scared that anything and everything is just mind-jarring. I know each of these because at one point or another, they have happened to me. Which is worse? Whichever one is happening at any given time is the worst one, because all of them are undesirable.

I want to know why I am so open about this thing I have. All my experiences and my limited outer knowledge of Asperger's has told me that people with it are tight-lipped about the issue. I certainly am not so, but why? My only thought on that is the fact that the pain is there all the time, so if I write or talk about it, it remains the same as if I were to just keep quiet.

Another thing I ponder about is the trade-off. In life, for every positive there seems to be a negative. My mom recently read some of my writings and said that she was so proud of me and that I have done more things than most people will do in an entire lifetime. That may be so, but at the same time there are some things I will *never* be able to experience even if money, time, or age were not issues. I have traveled the world, but a simple open conversation with my peer group is nearly impossible.

Imagine being able to do nearly everything you have ever wanted to do. I have been halfway around the world, driven multiple race cars, flown an airplane, and done numerous other non-normal activities, but I often ask myself if the trade-off is worth it. It is truly a double-edged sword. A set of paradoxes I have to live with. If I had a dollar for every paradox in my life, I'd at least be able to buy Boardwalk.

On one hand, I have an uncanny ability to recall information. The negative aspect of that is the annoyance it can cause to those around me. I know I can annoy my dad by correcting him on a statement he makes about something that happened a decade ago. I know the exact details, so I have no choice but to interrupt and make the correction. It doesn't take people long to learn this about me. A teammate in my bowling league asked me within four weeks, "Aaron, do you remember everything that has ever happened and then some?" Sadly, I do remember most everything that has happened to me, and I can recall it way too fast for my own good.

Another paradox is self-awareness. Some people have none, some have a little, and there are those few others who have too much. I believe I fall into the "too much" bracket. Again, there are two sides to this coin, and it is debatable if in the end it's better or worse. On the positive side, I am very hard to sway on issues (that is, if I tell you my stance on an issue), which means I hold firm in my beliefs.

On the other hand, it sometimes pains me to hear other people's opinions about issues when I have already made up my mind.

I wish more people could understand who I am. Anytime I mention Asperger's, people think it's a new vegetable or new diet trend. In other words, they have no earthly idea what the heck I am talking about. This goes straight to the heart because I know they will never fully grasp the pain and extreme heartache I feel every day. Maybe this is the reason I write. Maybe I am hoping that someday someone will read this and for a brief moment they will understand. Understanding is the only thing I want.

- - - - - - -

Last night I accomplished something on my invisible life-accomplishment list, bowling a game in excess of 297. My score wasn't perfect, but it was just a stick off—299. Near perfection, but whether it would have been a 298, 299, or 300, it didn't matter. I did it and I thought, *Okay, what does this mean?* I did get excited because of the ring I will be receiving, but other than that there was little satisfaction.

Could this be related to the closed-mindedness I mentioned earlier? I have observed from others that most people's best experiences come when shared with friends, but since I kept to myself during that game so much so most others around didn't even know I was going for the 300. And when you're isolated, your happiness is only as much as your mind will allow. I wish I could tell you how much that hurts.

Someone called me a word artist because I have been told that I can paint a vivid picture of what it's like to be me, but I know not how to describe the emptiness that should be filled with happiness. I have seen people throw

300s many times, and the jubilation on their faces is of such that if they were to die, they couldn't die happier. For me, besides the ring, there was nothing. Absolutely nothing.

What for most people is a lifetime achievement for me could be the most depressing thing of the month. Not because I did it, but because of the lack of feeling that I knew should have been there.

It's like walking into someone's living room for the first time. You would expect to see certain items—a couch, a television, and perhaps a phone are all things common in probably 99.9 percent of U.S. households. Now, let's say you go to someone's house and there's a couch facing an entertainment center, but no television. Your eye would catch that, and you might find it odd. That's how my brain is. I know that the proverbial television should be there, but for me, all I have is the entertainment center made of fine oak, no television. In this instance, the entertainment center would be very appealing, but no one buys an entertainment center as a stand-alone product. It is always bought to house the television. For me, the television symbolizes emotion that should be felt, and I *know* it should be felt, but there's just an empty space that is filled with nothing but air.

That's all the "I's" I have at the moment, but I know there has to be a sequel to this, because I's always come in twos, unless, of course, you're a Cyclops.

Finding Kansas

The Situational Handicap

Some people who know me and know that I have Asperger's think that there's nothing wrong with me. These people, however, see me only in certain situations and have no idea how paralyzed I can be in certain other situations. This can be very aggravating, because I know something isn't perfect with me, but when I hear such remarks as "Oh, you're fine" or "I can't see how you have that at all," it really bothers me.

To illustrate my point, let's say a person is paralyzed. However, for reasons unknown, this person is perfectly fine anytime they are in the state of Kansas. If you saw this person while in Kansas, you'd flat-out tell them, "Hey, you're not paralyzed!" At the time this comment would be true, but the person knows that the second he leaves the state he's paralyzed again.

Now, this person, knowing the magic of Kansas, would probably sell his home in whatever state he's in and move to Kansas so he would not be paralyzed. This is exactly how I try to be in life in regards to finding my Kansas.

When in my comfort zone, I am like that man in Kansas; there is nothing wrong, and I appear to be a normal individual. My ultimate Kansas is anything to do with racing. I am now the race director of two different series, and while at my post, I am firm and confident. These two traits can't be used to describe me very often in a social setting.

After the first race weekend this year, I went to a video game store to make a purchase. I walked into the store, making no eye contact with anyone, and was first asked the most horrifying question I know: "Sir, can I help you find something?" I instantly and passively said no, and a couple of seconds later I said the title of the game I would like to purchase. The store clerk, trying to make small talk, barraged me with several open-ended questions that I made closed-ended with simple yes or no answers. The clerk kept going, and he eventually said, "Umm, do you talk? I haven't gotten any words out of you!" As if I hadn't already known it, this was a clear confirmation (sorry for the cliché) that I wasn't in Kansas anymore.

This flip-flop difference can be very confusing for those around me. If my shadow could talk, it would certainly wonder how I can be the main guy at the racetrack but as passive as a sleeping kitten in a store setting.

As in the example, the guy would certainly want to live in the state that he can walk in. So, too, I want to do everything I can to not leave this magical state's limit. In simple terms, you could call this a comfort zone, but that phrase isn't strong enough. A comfort zone seems to describe a place that is just slightly better than a normal zone. In my life, it's more like a livable zone (Kansas) and a life-is-horrible-and-all-is-worthless zone (everything else). There is no comfort zone, no middle ground; it's either one or the other. Going into that game store, I wished so hard that the clerk would expedite the transaction because I didn't want to be put in that open-ended conversation that I knew I'd make closed-ended, and the awkwardness that comes with that is simply unbearable for me.

Let's say you're the paralyzed fellow. How would you feel if you're walking along by the state border and you venture into Oklahoma, and the instant you do you become paralyzed? One minute you are walking firmly and the next minute you are defenseless and helpless. One second you're self-sufficient and the next you have no ability to do anything. If this happened to you, even once, I'm sure you'd do everything you could to stay within Kansas.

Everyone has to do things they don't like. Most people have a tolerance, though, for these things. That example I used of the game store still hurts. Those open-ended questions with no meaning behind them have a significant meaning for me. I have to be crafty to survive each day. One solution I see to avoid this is to just purchase everything via the Internet.

What I want everyone to know is that this is situational handicap. I can be fine and dandy driving in the car somewhere, but when we get to the destination and there are other people, I am not who I was. From being able to run like an Olympian, I become as helpless as a bedridden invalid. Imagine the distress that comes with this. One minute I am like a person who has won the gold medal, and in an instant I become nothing more than an extra in a movie who has no lines while lying in a bed. I am seen but not heard.

With all this said, I do everything I can to stay in my state of Kansas. Being outside it is so unbearable that sometimes the question that comes to mind is, "Is life worth this?" The hardest part of all is when someone knows me only when I'm in my Kansas, and then they see me outside my livable state. It's like being completely naked and powerless to do anything. Whatever person this is has seen me firm and confident and now they see the true me. Once they see both sides, I'm sure they ask themselves what on earth is going on.

I know I refuse to do many things with people because of all these facts. I hope they realize, though, that being outside my state, I feel like life isn't worth living. It's like having two choices—running like the wind or being stationary and blind. Like anyone's answer, I'd choose to run like the wind.

But when I'm in Kansas, I don't just run. I fly.

Music

I used to ask Aaron why he listened to this song or that song.
I didn't understand why he would never answer. As this essay
reveals, sometimes it is not rudeness or rebellion that causes
this type of silence.

In school, I always loathed music talk because I knew the
"What music do you listen to?" question would come up.
Every time I would skate around the issue. What was worse
than answering the question was the part of thinking about
the answer. This pattern has steadily gotten worse as I have
gotten older. So what on earth is the problem here?

Enter Aaron's music theory. This theory isn't boring like
talking about half notes and treble clefs all day, but rather
the thought process and near-disabling effect music has.

If I were typical, I would assume that music is just that:
music. However, for me, music is much deeper than notes

and instruments. It is almost a direct path straight into the memory core of my brain. When one song comes to mind, another pops up, and then another, and so on and so on.

Take, for instance, my drive through the Rockies west of Denver. At the time I had a CD playing that I'd created. Attached to the songs that were playing, and permanently etched into my brain, was each and every quarter mile of I-70. Another example is that morning in Lithuania when I heard the song from a video game. Hearing that song today instantly reminds me of my surroundings in that hotel.

For me, music is a scary and unknown entity. But, of course, the question I haven't asked is why am I so private about my music choices. That would seem to be a hard question to answer, but I have an answer that requires no second thought. It's simply that I don't want to think about music. To think about it is to put me right back to a time or place that I heard a song, and then I instantly remember all the emotions, sights, smells, and everything else associated with it.

Could this be related to "firsts"? It very well could be. The songs that are most significant are those that I have heard while a new "first" is in process.

But now, back to the privacy issue: Let's say someone asked me if I liked Cher's "Believe." I will instantly become frozen, because I don't think about the actual song, but rather the time frame that I remember hearing it. Sure, a song can be heard many times innocently without a second thought. But when something special happens and a song is playing, the two get linked like a very special chemical bond. The song mentioned above was playing when I bowled my first nonleague 300 while working at the bowling alley. So, if someone does ask me about the song, I instantly try my best not to recall the first time I heard it. But it never works, and I go back in time to the place where I heard it.

The association of that Cher song then takes me right back to that hot summer night in 2000 working a Wednesday that saw zero paid bowlers. It was practically empty, so Carol let me bowl until patrons showed up. The scores I threw are irrelevant because that's not what I remember. What I remember is those nights working and being content with my surroundings at that time. What I then remember is the short-term future of that memory and the nights coming home and playing my retro gaming systems and all the life discoveries I made during that summer. All of that comes to mind from just the simple question of whether or not I like that song.

Why this happens, I don't know, but what I do know is that somewhere there is a very tight bond in my brain that helps music cripple me.

I am truly overloaded while I write this because I am reliving so many things by just mentioning this effect music has on me. One could say that with my memory, my life has been scored musically. A soundtrack of my life, one could say.

In a movie, music has a big effect on the viewer. It is debatable as to whether or not the movie *Jaws* would have had the same impact had it not been for that famous, spine-tingling theme. The movie *Titanic* certainly would not have had the same emotional impact had it not been for its resounding theme. What if that same principle held true outside the movie theater?

If I tell someone I like a song, for me it's like exposing my most important memories. To give that much away is to give them the keys to my car, house, or, heck, why don't I just give them my Social Security number so they can steal my identity?

For me, music is more than just notes; it is my life and the gateway to all my memories, and I don't want anyone to fully understand the link for every song, so if I say, "I don't know," don't take offense. But realize that the answer I give is just like clothes: they hide what lies beneath, and if you know what songs I like, I am virtually emotionally naked in your eyes.

Travel

For as many bad things that have happened to me while traveling, I have also had a lot of good experiences, and for that I am grateful. I do realize that a very small percentage of people my age have traveled as many miles as I have. This could be an important part of why I am still sane.

But what do I mean by sane? There is something really odd that happens to me when traveling to a destination that isn't home. It is a feeling of liberation and pure freedom. All prior stressors and mental clutter are gone and my mind is at ease.

When I am on a long car ride, it is like having the recycle bin in my brain emptied. For me, when at home under normal circumstances, my mind is constantly thinking. Even when there's nothing to think about, my mind will stress about the fact that there is currently nothing to think about. After a while, that gets really old! But there are so many stimuli when traveling. Driving for twelve hours in any direction will generate many miles of things to think about. Colors of cars, beautiful landscape, and crossing a state line are all examples of some of the minor thrills that make traveling so liberating.

Through all the chaos of the noise of the road, the constant hum of the motor, and the ever-changing scenery comes the most tranquil feeling I know. I do find it odd that something that is so taxing on the senses is one of the most tranquil and peaceful feelings I experience.

For what long car rides do for me, long flights and long layovers do even more. As they say, "Half the fun is getting there." For me, it's more like, "All the fun is traveling to and from wherever I am going." It is very odd that something that many people don't like is one of the most, if not *the* most, peaceful times I know. The long layovers are so nice. Maybe it's the fact that you *have* to sit and *wait* and there's nothing you can do about it. This goes for a long drive as well. Unlike a day in my hometown, a long drive is quite structured, and the matter of the day is not done until the destination is reached.

It's very much like a sporting event. If you go to a baseball game, you know that a regulation game is nine innings; if you go to a soccer match, you know regulation time is ninety minutes. For a long drive, you will know that if you've gone fifty miles on a five-hundred-mile trip, you are one-tenth of the way there.

Driving down the road in a car is like being on another planet, cut off from all other human interaction for three hundred miles at a time (when you stop for gas). Thoughts regarding money, other people, the future, and the like are gone, vanished from my mind.

Maybe the feeling I have while traveling is what it's like to be normal. To be able to have a clear mind and not over-think about the importance of an irrelevant fact or emotion. Perhaps this is the true reason travel is the supreme bliss I know.

Another thing that is so blissful is the constant change of the cast of characters. When I travel with my dad, the only constant is him, and the world and the other people are always changing. Because of this, my shortcomings and the way people may look at me or think I am different are gone.

On a plane ride, it's like there are just two hundred people left in the world. All communication is essentially cut off for the passengers. The outside world is just a speck on the ground, and everything that was stressful is miles away.

Is this an example of running away from a problem? The answer is no. While it may look like it is, it is not, because during the process of getting to a destination, my mind can make sense of the world and not get overloaded.

I always look forward to a long trip. The short time I get to experience normality can't be simulated by any other activity. Because of this, in the back of my mind I always want to say, "Please tell me that we're not there yet and that we're miles and miles away from our destination so I can enjoy this feeling just a bit longer."

What *Has* Become . . . ?

In all the choices I have made in my life, I have always been under the impression that I will be able to see what has become of everything. Time and time again, though, I am left in the dark. What has become of people I used to know? Where is the epilogue that I expected to see?

But why am I under such an impression? This question has rattled through my brain many times with no clear answer. That is, until I thought of my "firsts" theory and movies at the same time.

Nearly every movie or television show these days ties up all the loose ends by the time the movie or show is over. Commonplace are sequences of what happened after the story, where the characters are now, if they were based on a real person, and 99 percent of the time there is complete closure of the story. This, too, occurs in most story-based video games.

It's almost an obsession how movies tie loose ends. I

don't think it used to be that way, though. In the few books I've read that weren't from this century or the last, I noticed the endings are often sudden and vague. Imagination is needed to complete the story. It's not handed to you on a silver platter. "What happened next?" is not answered. Flash forward to today and very few TV shows or movies leave you asking that question in the end.

"What has become . . . ?" is a question I have asked many times these past four years. I never realized, though, that in life answers aren't readily available to that question. If my theory of "firsts" is true, then a child who watches movies or television may pick up on the expectation that one will nearly always know how the story ends.

So I learned that the end isn't really the end. That concept isn't very dangerous when you're five. As a child grows older, however, if this concept isn't overridden by experiences, there will be a problem.

The truly painful thing is that this problem is a reminder of what I have. It isn't the person I miss, but the *facts* that I don't know. I don't know what happens next in their story. In other words, it's not them at all. It is another example of my incapability to feel emotions toward others.

I don't know if you can imagine what this feels like. On the one hand, I have the immense pain of not knowing how they are. On the other hand, I realize it isn't them I am feeling pain about. To know that I am unable to grieve over the loss of a friend is tragic. To realize the real pain is in the knowledge I have lost is about the worst pain I can feel. It totally destroys my self-esteem because it makes me feel

Finding Kansas

cold and heartless, since in those movies and television shows, it never played out like that.

This distorted logic is quite dangerous because the question of "What has become . . . ?" can be applied to anything. I often wonder what became of that aluminum can I have written about on several occasions, or the flight attendant on the flight from Lithuania to Poland who smiled way too much, or the bellhop from the hotel in Kenya, or a dollar bill I may have had in my wallet for a month. The possibilities are endless.

It's hard to live life while constantly being dragged into the past with those questions. It's much like a driving a car. If you are constantly looking in the rearview mirror, you cannot see where you're going, and then you won't recognize the objects in the mirror because you didn't notice them while you were moving forward, so then you are always a step, or many steps, behind. Me, I'm years behind. By the way, "Whatever became of the . . . ?"

Fear Versus Fear

One of the best baseball games of all time took place in 2005 during the National League Division Series. Atlanta and Houston were deadlocked after some heroics on Houston's part. What happened after the heroics was a marathon of scoreless baseball. What started as an afternoon affair turned into a game that saw the arrival of dusk. Chris Burke broke the tie in the bottom of the eighteenth with a walk-off home run and ended the longest play-off game of all time.

Let's say, though, that all the players were so tired that no one had the strength to hit a home run, much less swing the bat. The game would be in equilibrium and neither side would have the chance to win, making the game go on forever. Granted, a team would eventually run out of arms on the mound and someone would eventually hit a ball long enough, but in this instance, let's say that wouldn't happen. Both sides would be exhausted and nobody would be able to win, making the game last forever.

This is what it's like for me when it comes to many things, including work. Neither side of my fears can win. The interesting thing about the two fears is that if one would prevail, the other would be taken care of. Instead of being taken care of, though, they are currently in the 105th inning of play.

So what are the two fears? One of them is the much-repeated topic of money. The other one is the fear of the pain of working in society.

Let's talk about the money fear first (fear A). So far in the second half of this year, I have made some money to get to my goal of what I would be comfortable with, or so I thought. After nearly a year and a half chasing that goal I achieved it, but the fear didn't go away. In fact, the anxiety increased by an alarming amount. Instead of fearing having zero dollars and not having the goal, I now have double the fear of zero dollars and triple the fear of falling below the safe level.

As I have mentioned before, it is always something. There is always something that my mind will obsess on and worry about. What is truly interesting, I believe, is the fact that I was more comfortable having little money. Now that I have it, I worry about losing it. I tend to look at the big picture (referring to time and future), so the only thing I can see is expenditures and not possible income.

On the flip side is the fear of the workplace (fear B). (I think it should be noted that when I use the word "fear," I don't mean it as, say, a fear of spiders or rabid rhinos from the zoo that may escape but rather the deepest fear that one can have, internal fear.) If I were able to work, the fear of money would be negated because there would always be income. On paper this seems really easy, because logic would dictate that if this fear was broken, all would be fine and dandy.

It's not that easy, though. The multitude of stressors at a job is too much to bear. These include socializing, the irrelevance of being perfect, and the time. Every day I wish I could be in the normal crowd and just live with it so that both fears would dissolve away.

So those are the two fears that are battling it out now in the 106th inning. Neither side is willing to throw in the towel, and the cruel game continues. To be stuck in this way is aggravating beyond belief. To realize that it would be so easy to conquer fear B and that would dissolve fear A. But at this point the two are engaged in this eternal tie game. The deep sadness that fear A gives me is equal to what fear B causes me. In other words, just like the opponents in the play-off game, they are equal.

I've had this epic battle of fears for as long as I can remember. Even in school I thought of this. It was a bit different since fear B would represent school instead of the workplace, but I still feared money. I was always told that one must go to school so they can make more money, but the pain of school made for the first game of fear versus fear.

Time progressed, and I got a job at a bowling alley. I wasn't affected too much at the time, because I was sixteen and ahead of the game. I wasn't forced to be there, and it really wasn't a job, but rather getting ahead. However, as with many other things in my life, time progressed and I did not. From getting ahead to falling behind was quite painful. People I knew were going to college and, as I was told, college means money. But yet again, these evenly matched fears would not allow me to move forward. So here I am now, stuck in the middle with the game, about to go to the 107th inning. By this time in the game, all the fans have left, and even the television network has cut away. The players are all alone. With the pain that being stuck in this game has brought, so am I.

Sentence

A sentence is a scary thing. Not the type of sentence that is written on a computer or with pen and paper, but rather the type convicts receive. Outside of the death penalty, the highest of sentences is the life sentence. When the felon hears the verdict of a life sentence, his life is changed forever. Everything before is irrelevant because for the rest of his life he will not be free. I didn't commit a crime, but the day I was told that I have Asperger's was very much like a gavel crashing down, finalizing my fate.

Before my sentence, I always knew I was a bit different. I always thought it was just because I was smarter and more mature than others my age. I always thought that my rigidity came from the fact that I firmly knew I was right and everyone else was wrong. Little did I know the truth that it wasn't them, but me.

After I learned the truth, I slid into a deep depression. Knowing what I had made me think that all my life was going to be like a train on tracks in that I would be unable to deviate from where the tracks take me. The tracks are the limitations of Asperger's.

Not only was it hard for me, but it was surprisingly hard for Emily, whom I was involved with at the time I was diagnosed. At first she wanted to hear none of it. "You'll never be able to like me!" and, "You can never change nor accept me," were some of the things she said to me. Not only had I been sentenced but with it came solitary confinement.

In the end, her comments sealed the deal and resulted in the end of our relationship. When I needed someone the most, I was alone. This was a "first" in that I thought no one could like me because of what I have. My mind believed that solitary would last forever.

With the sentence came the knowledge that normality would always elude me. Love? Forget about it. Not having weird little obsessions? Ha! Friends? Get used to spending evenings with reruns on television. The sentence is about the most depressing thing I can think of because it holds no hope. And to know what I am missing is the worst feeling I think anyone can feel. I've heard people say phrases such as "All you need is love" and "Friends are what make the day worthwhile," but neither one of those phrases can apply to me.

Time has progressed, and I have often wondered how things would be if I didn't know. They say, "What you don't know can't hurt you," but this raises the logical and relevant question of just who "they" really are. Finding out why I am what I am was very important. If I had never known,

I believe there would be more self-hatred, because instead of blaming a syndrome, I would blame myself.

Finding out about it has changed my life forever. The sentence was read to me by a doctor, but even if I had never found out, I would still have a soul and be an Asperger's sufferer walking.

Crippled in Addiction

Addictions can be extremely debilitating. From drinking to gambling, there are organizations that exist to help people with their addictions. But what if a person can be addicted to anything?

Everything I do is done based on an addiction. I don't do anything unless I'm addicted to it. Perhaps the word "obsession" is better suited rather than addiction, but "addiction" is a stronger and more powerful word, and furthermore, obsessions aren't always viewed as a negative. For me, addictions are crippling.

If people do everything that they are addicted to, then they could not do new things. For me, one of the addictions is the routine of things. If I do something one way the first time, I must do it that way the second, and every time thereafter, from stopping at a particular diner before an annual sporting event, down to the routine weekly and daily details of life. To *not* do it that way—the first way—is unthinkable.

The scope of my addictions, though, goes further than just routine. The repetitive thoughts I have don't disappear. Money, global politics, and the idiocy of why there is no Interstate 50 are just some of the thoughts that keep going around and around.

Let's say I got a job at a different bank. First thing is, it wouldn't be the old bank. Second, I'd have to meet new people. Third, I would start thinking about the possibility of being robbed and shot. Don't tell me that this is a self-fulfilling prophecy because I am already starting to think about that and I haven't even filled out an application. This feeling of being stuck in the middle of two addictions is downright crippling. And not only crippling, but it constantly delivers blows to my self-esteem that a heavyweight fighter would be proud of fending off.

An addiction can be anything and everything. Back when I lived with my mom and worked at a bowling alley, I would always play the same video games when I got home. And about 50 percent of the time, my mom would want to talk or have me do some irrelevant chore that could easily be taken care of in the morning. This created extreme friction because she was hindering me from doing what I wanted. At the time, I did not realize why I got so mad but now I do. It was that I was addicted to what I was doing. This trend of being interrupted is still around. Ask my dad how reliable I am at taking out the trash or a pizza box if he asks me to do it while I'm doing something else.

What is it about being interrupted that is so aggravating that I could literally get so angry that I could break something? Just the small thing of someone closing a door can break my mode of thought to the degree that I want to scream. I constantly tell myself that it isn't a big deal, but then I'm just lying to myself because to everyone else it isn't a big deal but to me it is strong enough to raise my pulse to the point I can feel the blood flowing through my fingertips.

Perhaps a good analogy would be a train. They do call it a train of thought (has anyone seen the real "they," because they say lots of things?) and when a door shuts or I am asked to do something, it is like taking out ten feet of track; when the train gets there, it makes for a spectacular derailment.

This is sad to realize because I know how stuck up or snobbish I sound. What gives me the right to deem a task stupid? Why should I have gotten upset when my mom wanted to talk? Why do I get so upset when someone closes the door to the room where I write this? The answer is, I have no power to say no, but that doesn't change the fact that I feel so much anxiety when any of those things happen.

When derailed from an addiction, I get so angry that all of life is deemed nearly irrelevant. Depression, anxiety, anger, animosity, and self-hatred are all experienced. Most of the time, my brain is like one of those bullet trains in Japan. In other words, it is going really fast, and my brain likes it that way. But when something out of the routine intrudes, it knocks that speeding train right off the tracks, and then my thoughts aren't in that controlled environment that most addictions provide.

I get especially angry when it involves tardiness. One time when I went to pick up Emily, she was ten minutes late getting out of the house; those ten minutes were ten minutes of pure loathing. Although the time I was surrounded by homeless boys in Kenya was dangerous, the mental trauma brought on by sitting in my car and waiting was greater. Think about that. A life-threatening ordeal was not as bad to my overall psychological well-being as sitting in a car in a comfortable climate with nothing remotely life-threatening happening.

My least favorite day in school was always the topsy-turvy day. This was when the regular order of the day was thrown out and the next class was determined by a draw. Not knowing what class was next was like stopping an addiction cold turkey. These days only occurred in second and seventh grade, but I made sure to do everything in my power to avoid going to school on those days.

Now I have to mention the racing aspect. A race car driver is always traveling. Drivers may have a race in Phoenix during the day, and by midnight that night they are back home in North Carolina. I can't think of a better life than that. Through the madness of constant change comes sameness. I know this is true because this is what international travel has been like for me. There isn't enough time for a "constant" addiction to occur; therefore, I am free. I'm sure my dad would say I am somewhat different on trips, and this is the reason why.

There is addiction in my writing style as well. I always

use the same font type for the title and then for the actual piece. I have tried to change it just for the sake of change but am unable to.

I don't know of a solution to this problem. My brain is wired to the point that to take these away would be almost like removing Windows from a computer. Yes, you'd still have the computer, but with no operating system it would be useless. I wish it were as simple as just switching to Linux, but that would be just too easy, wouldn't it? And then there's the fear of learning a new OS, and what happens if it malfunctions and their customer support team isn't good, and what if . . .

Must . . .

For me, there are certain thoughts that reach obsessive levels that don't go away and the only way out is to just do them.

"I must think of a way to make money" is a common "must." I must think about it. Beyond the fact of thinking about *how* to make the money, I think about the process of *must* thinking about money. It's like spyware on a computer. Your computer may be running properly, but hiding deep within is a program that is silently running and that, at a moment's notice, produces a pop-up ad on your screen.

These near-obsessive thoughts are vigorous in their pursuit to make whatever their objective is done. Maybe it's a spurt of OCD, but whatever the case, there is *no* known way in my mind to break the cycle when it starts.

This can easily be tied into "firsts." Once a thought comes into the mind, it is there for good, and the only way to end it is to achieve whatever the must is. One of the two examples I'll use is my mission to become the number one racer on *Project Gotham Racing 3*, more commonly known as *PGR3*.

PGR3 was a launch title for the Xbox 360. Previously, I had been number one on three other racing games and my mind was set on making this the fourth game that would see me as number one in the world. You could say that it is motivation that is pushing me to get there, or pure desire, but neither is the case. The *only* reason is that I *must* get number one. There is no alternative to this. Number one is the only option and nothing else will do.

When I got the game, I adapted quickly to it and the new console. I got the system four days late, which meant many people had a leg up on me, so I needed to learn quickly and I did so. I quickly moved into the top one hundred, top fifty, and after a week, I cracked the top ten.

In online games there is a "lag" factor. With so many servers and Xboxes communicating with one another, there is always the risk that a person may "lag out," meaning their connection is severed and they are dropped from the race. The person who is so unfortunate will see on his screen that everyone quit the race when in reality, he was the only one who dropped out. The main race will finish and the driver who lagged out will take last place and lose a lot of points to everyone else because the system will think that the driver quit.

When I cracked the top ten I hadn't suffered a lag out, but my luck was up. One lag out and I dropped from tenth to sixteenth. Shortly thereafter, another lag out dropped me from fourteenth to twenty-third. This was devastating! I was good enough to be number one, and circumstances outside my control were preventing me from getting there. Oddly, I felt the most anger toward myself. The thought was that I must be number one, but with this lagging out, I'd be unable to, but even so, I *must* be on top for no other reason than to just be there. It's not to prove that I am the best, or good, but simply because I must do it.

Because of that driving force that is "must," that is the equivalent of a mile-long coal train traveling downhill at fifty-five miles per hour. I kept at it, and twenty-third became twentieth, became fifteenth, then back to where I was before the lag outs began. With me recovering, I went on a winning tear and cracked the top five within a day and a half. I got up to fourth, and the top three was in sight.

One thing you must know is that the rating system is called TrueSkill. It was developed by two professors at the University of Cambridge and is loosely based on the chess ELO system. Because of this, the interval between third and fourth is much greater than it is from eighty-ninth to nine-tieth. When I say much greater, it is much like the Richter scale in that a 7.0 earthquake is nowhere near as strong as an 8.0. That being said, when I got to third, it was a mile-stone. Now there were just two spots left, and I *had to* over-take those two spots.

The next day I worked at it and got to second. I was now within one spot of the position I must be in. Then fate dealt a cruel blow: a lag out. Then, if that wasn't bad enough, fifteen minutes later it happened again. I fell from second to ninth. How could this happen? I was so close! The feelings I felt were of deep, deep rage. I constantly hit the arm of the chair with enough force to sprain my left hand. With the "must" I had in my mind, there was no option other than to be first, and now it seemed like it would be impossible.

I regrouped and again went on a winning streak like no other. From ninth I went to seventh, seventh turned to fourth, and I was back at the penultimate position. I knew the gap between second and first prior to me taking second was like the gap between New York and London. I worked and worked and finally I got what I set out to do and I was number one. But now what?

Was there joy? There was a little, but nothing much. The obsessive "must" thoughts were put to ease, but what was left was a void. Literally, my mind thought, *Now what?* I worked and I worked and I worked at it and I got it, but unlike the runners in the New York City marathon that have a fanfare at the finish, I had nothing except a number one by my name.

Perhaps in the obsessive nature of having to get first, the rareness and greatness of that spot's meaning is lost. Anyone who is in the medium skill level would probably give an arm or a leg, or maybe in the least a hundred dollars, just to be number one for a day. There are more than fifty thousand people and I was number one. Skill might have gotten me there, but there was no other option because I *must* be in that spot.

"I must" isn't isolated to global domination of a video game. It can be as minor as wanting a candy bar just because I might need to eat it five days later. A quick example could be the sunflower seeds I eat. I have a tub that has several bags' worth in it. If I were to eat an hour a day, there would be at least a week's worth in it. I keep a couple of bags in reserve just in case I run out. At two a.m. last Friday, I used my last reserve bag and I literally panicked. While I had a week's worth in my tub, there was no reserve. So I got my shoes on and in the middle of the night I went to the store to buy more just in case I ran out.

Somewhere in my life I was taught that I always need a reserve. This is where "firsts" and "musts" meet. The "first" is needing the reserve; therefore, I must have the three extra bags. The two may seem the same, but they are separate entities, albeit intertwined with each other.

The final example I'll use is of this game I bought today. For the Xbox, I bought (please don't laugh) *Karaoke Revolution Party*. As the name implies, it is a karaoke game. You play with a microphone, and it uses voice recognition to know if you are on pitch or not. The game has fifty songs, but I looked on the game's downloadable content and saw that for a certain price you could download one hundred more. If you read about the sunflower seeds, you already know about the conflict to come.

I hadn't played the game yet, but I knew there were more songs. Immediately, I must have those extras, but what about the price? "It will drop me close to my limit I don't want to drop below, but I need, no, must have it, but the cost, but I *must!*" is a clip of the constant barrage of bantering that went on.

In the end, I could not withhold the urge and I purchased the additional song packs even though I could've in the future when I'll play the game and have more money.

Both primary examples, while completely different, are of the same nature. Once the mind is set, there is *no* alternative. I feel that the musts are a stem of firsts. Firsts are the rules that the mind lives by, and the musts carry out the rules. Yes, this makes perfect sense in the *PGR3* case. The first I learned is that I need to be in first (I believe I picked that up in school because in most everything I always was so); therefore, I *must* be in first. When such expectations exist, there can be *no* joy in getting there because it is expected, and when something is expected it is of little relevance because that's "just the way it is supposed to be."

Impulsive buying remains somewhat of a mystery to me. Once I learn of a product I want, my mind will not stop until the product is in hand. I'm sure retailers love that mentality, but I know I do not. Perhaps the collectible market racket's clients all have Asperger's, because they all *must* purchase the next product.

Musts stem further than those two examples. When in a new conversation I must get the upper hand and have most of the control so perhaps racing can be talked about. Musts are the results of firsts and could be the survival mechanism that keeps the mind on track. As unbreakable as a first is, a must is even more so. Firsts taught me so.

The Hazards of "Firsts"

As I wrote in the previous chapter, the "must" attitude stems from firsts. You could almost call the *must* the judge, jury, and executioner of the law created by the firsts. This can be very good, but it also can be very, *very* bad.

All aspects of my life are dictated by "firsts." The firsts are the groundwork for who I am, and the musts are the things that keep everything in line. This can be bad because a must is very hard to ignore.

This concept of firsts keeps getting scarier for me because, if musts are true, an Asperger's mind is much like a game of Jenga. If you play the game right, the tower of blocks will be steady, but all it takes is just one missing block for the tower to come crashing down.

I've read and heard that many people with Asperger's have just one interest. This is the biggest security blanket and further proves my point. If a person has just one field of interest, change will be minor. I've also heard that those fields are normally in a safe and constant environment; therefore, the firsts and musts can be played out with little to no interference.

Interference—any minor change in the way things are supposed to be, based on my firsts—is a very discomforting event for me.

One of the major interferences that come about is the breaking of rules. Let's take Monopoly for an example. I will fight tooth and nail to keep in force the 10 percent interest fee to get back-mortgaged from the bank. "Oh, that's a stupid rule," is a comment often heard, but it's in the rules and it's been that way since 1935. I do have some "house rules," as they are called. Minor tweaks that are added to the game, but the ones I have are perfect, and at another person's house I will not bend on my rules. To do so is to create a rift in the order of things.

If a game of Monopoly can be canceled just because of these firsts and musts, think of the bigger things that could happen. Marriages destroyed, violent outbursts, and loss of life come to mind. I believe these could be avoided; however, a near-perfect environment has to be preserved, and, as we all know, life is far from perfect.

With that being so, it's becoming clearer and clearer to me why one with Asperger's may have an obsessive fascination with a certain brand of car. A 1955 Chevy will always be a 1955 Chevy. Whoever designed it then will always have the credit of designing it, the number produced will never change, and every other aspect of that brand will always be constant. The same thing goes for any other his-

torical oddity like trains, planes, presidents, the 1911 baseball season, and so on.

As I have mentioned, when the internal compass gets
derailed, bad things happen. What can be done? Parenting
is the first and foremost important field of defense. Parents
themselves can't change what the firsts and musts become,
but they can prevent certain ones from forming. Also, trying to change ones that are planted could lead to rebellion
or fits of outrage.

I can remember back when I was seven, I had a dentist
appointment at eight p.m. on a Saturday. Yes, I know it was
an odd time for an appointment, but it was made worse because it was the Saturday that NASCAR has their night race
at Bristol. To make matters even worse, I would be able to
watch the start of the race before I would be forced, against
my will, to go to the dentist. I can remember telling the dentist that he should hurry so I could get home. When he
came back with the snippy comment of, "That isn't a way a
good patient would act. Don't you want to be a good little
patient?" I snapped. I remember crying aloud. Why didn't
he understand? *Bristol was on and I was missing it!* I told him
a race was on and he was completely clueless that they even
raced on Saturday night. This confused me. Why didn't he
know, and furthermore, *why wasn't he hurrying?*

As you can tell by the emphasis, this was a very heated
moment for me. This is the type of interference that I'm
talking about. Racing was implanted in my mind as a first;
therefore, I must watch the race as it happens, and this dentist didn't have the foggiest of idea of the need I had to get

home. I'm sure my parents were confused over this strong desire to miss that appointment and the severity of stress it caused me.

That type of scene is probably repeated day in and day out with little to no thought as to why a seven-year-old can want something that seems irrelevant so badly. Therefore, as I said, parents are the first line of defense. If they are aware of this tightrope walk, scenes like this can be minimized. Had I not had good parents, that outburst could have been repeated, but with worse consequences, again and again.

Interference can't be avoided. I'm thankful that I realize this fact. Otherwise, I would easily fall off the tightrope and plummet to whatever lies below. However, when musts are interfered with constantly, there can be no balance good enough to keep me on the wire.

As long as a hazard is known, it can be dealt with. Parents who are unaware could literally drive their kid/teen/young adult to death trying to help when they are actually doing the complete opposite of what the child needs for balance on the tightrope.

The only defense for families is knowledge. The family will not be able to change the individual, but they may be able to change the individual's future that so it is much brighter and happier.

Media and "Firsts"

This is an obvious comment: we are constantly bombarded by media. Print, radio, and television are just a few. In fact, some people wake up to the media via their alarm clocks. In a perfect world, this isn't a bad thing. Add Asperger's to the equation and things get a bit tricky, as well as possibly dangerous. Why do I believe it is dangerous? To start, we must go back more than one hundred years.

One hundred years ago, survival was paramount. People didn't worry about missing a television show; people weren't listening to music countdowns. There was only one thing that mattered: survival. Having food, shelter, and other life essentials were the "firsts" that most people experienced and carried around with them.

Let's flash forward to today. Knowledgeable five-year-olds in a middle-class home may have multiple forms of open-ended media at their disposal—video games, television, and the open-ended universes of the Internet. The amount of information at anyone's fingertips is mind-boggling, and for someone who may take many "first" snapshots, it is too many.

Twenty-five years ago, video games were limited to arcades that were primarily teenage hangouts. Today with the Xbox, Wii, and portable systems, a video game can be played nearly anywhere. If a first is developed, there may be no other world for a child with Asperger's except within the game. Since the child probably doesn't have to worry about starving to death, the game becomes life. With this being so, why would the child need social interaction? They wouldn't need it because they don't know it.

With the example above, the child learned to play the game, and since it became a first, it won't leave. What's the point of everything else if only the game matters? Using that logic, what would the point of anything be if it doesn't include the video games? This is a small example, and I think that this one-track mind can be expanded to include anything and everything. Much like a computer programmed for one and only one function, so, too, is this child who takes a devout interest in video games.

Television, too, is a scary medium. For a child with Asperger's, TV is a barrel full of firsts that can destroy a child's way of thought.

If a family watches the news, the child with Asperger's

will quickly learn of the evil in the world and quickly hate everyone because of the death factor. It used to be that a child learned about death through the loss of a grandparent but now, turn on the news and you will hear of a suicide bomber in the Middle East, a murder-suicide in New York, a workplace shooting downtown, a small plane crash in the mountains, and the list goes on and on.

A century ago, the world for most people ended on the street corner. This would be ideal for an Asperger's person because the dangers and evil would be unknown. Now, though, we live in a global community where all the dangers of the world are known. For a child with Asperger's, this is very, *very bad*. I can remember at the outset of Desert Storm asking repeatedly, "But why will they fight, and why will people die, and will it happen here?" I think I was fortunate in the fact that I was able to express this concern; had I not, those fears would have festered and gotten worse over time.

TV also affects interpersonal relationships. If firsts can be established at any age, it leads us to believe that a murder and a coworker romance conflict can be cured in one hour or less minus those all-important commercials. They cannot, under most circumstances, but if the first has been laid down, it becomes confusing as to why not.

The worst thing about the current forms of media is that they are almost impossible to avoid. For a normal person, these can be enjoyable half-hour escapes from the stress of daily life. For a person with Asperger's, it can be the bible on which all life experiences will be based. When the real world hits, there is no reset button, no power button, and the channel can't be changed. The sad thing is, there may be no understanding as to why everything won't be wrapped up before the eleven o'clock news.

Future

If there is one thing more frightening to me than anything else in the entire universe, it is the future. They say that if you don't know history, you're bound to make the same mistakes. Well, that's fine and all, but that does nothing for what might or might not happen in five, fifteen, or twenty-five minutes. Could there be a phone call? What if it says that the number is unlisted? Will the doorbell ring? Who will be at the door? I ask all the above questions every second of every day, for questions as simple as the time of dinner to as major as what I will be doing in a year's time.

All the time and effort my mind puts in trying to calculate the future takes a major toll on my overall psyche. In most cases, I am comfortable only when I am able to predict the outcome. To make a simple analogy, it would be like a small child's toy that when you press a button, it makes a noise. Before the button is pressed, there would be great anxiety because I wouldn't know what exactly would happen, but after one time, it becomes like second nature.

That analogy works great on simple things, but one must remember that I try to figure out what *everything* will be. Let's do some math . . .

There're 60 seconds in a minute and 60 minutes in an hour and 24 hours in a day, making the week 168 hours long. Now to make the true pain of my mind known, let's multiply 60 seconds by 60 minutes; then we see that there are 3,600 seconds in an hour, and now that total times 24 hours gets us 86,400 seconds in just one day. Every second I am up, I am constantly telling myself what's going to happen next. When the current next comes and goes, there's another one, and another one, and it just keeps going on like that.

This is why I wish life were more like chess. Chess is bound by the rules of movement. A bishop can only move diagonally on whichever color it started on, a king can only move one space in direction, and so on and so forth. Life, however, is like the queen in that she can move in any direction at any distance on any given turn so long as there's a straight line. If every piece within the game of chess were allowed this movement, with so many possibilities and variables, it would be all-out chaos. Just like life.

One Thousand Outcomes

Everyday life can go in a thousand directions. The car breaking, the lottery being won, donkeys invading any baseball game, and a helicopter landing in your front yard are just some of the nearly infinite possibilities each day brings. These events are of major proportion, but for me thinking of big things isn't as big as thinking of each possibility of small things.

In most social circumstances I would consider myself to be a bit slow. It isn't that I'm dumb and uncommunicative; it's just the opposite. What's going on in my brain is trying to figure out any of the thousand outcomes that may come from the next sentence I'm going to use. Okay, so it may not be a thousand, but regardless of the number, it's way too many.

This would explain why I'm nearly normal when it's a one-on-one conversation, but if one extra person gets added, I become silent. It's simple math. Let's say I'm talking to one person, so therefore in my thinking, the thoughts are a multiple of one. If we throw in one more person, not only does the multiple go to two, but it goes to three, because not only do I have to try to calculate how the second person is going to react, but now I have to think about how the first person is going to react to the second person. Did I say this was simple math? My mistake. If we throw in a third person, the math becomes such that someone could go for his or her doctorate in mathematics trying to solve that equation.

That was the conversation example, but this type of thinking applies to everything. It gets down to the simplest level of seeing a guy walk toward my car. As I watch him, I begin to wonder if he will smash my window. Will he pull a gun? Will another car hit him? As my mind goes through these motions, it's as if time freezes in the real world while I try to calculate all the scenarios. With all this going on, rarely, if ever, is the fear of the person actualized. But that's what's always happened.

Having a mind like this is exhausting. Nothing is ever a quick decision, but it's almost a requirement to try to predict what's going to happen before it happens (which it usually never does). This lowers my ability to clearly think when something actually does happen. This can be quite bad because when something that is completely from left field happens, I go into mental shock and I have no idea how to react.

This thought process of a thousand outcomes wouldn't be bad if all I had to deal with was putting gas in my car. What can go wrong? Well, at least I know how to dial 911.

Dealing with people, there could be one billion outcomes. So, as much as I try to prepare, I'm only going to get it right a very small percentage of the time.

You can't practice for the unpredictable, and what separates the great from the not so great in life is how one reacts to the unpredicted. (When I say "great" I'm not referring to great leaders or great inventors, but rather to the people who live life with happiness, because I see that as true greatness.) I react very poorly because, at first, I don't react at all. Then, when enough has happened, I'll do everything in my power to rid myself of whatever has given me too much unpredictability.

This affects all aspects of life because everything will eventually throw a curveball at some point in time. Using my math formula, it's no wonder I detested school so much. If there are one thousand outcomes for one person, and one thousand times one thousand times one thousand for three people, I don't even want to imagine the mathematical nightmare that is a full classroom. And if that formula is scary on paper, try to think what it is like living with it!

There is no slowing down this outcome process because I need it to keep my sanity. As tiring as trying to think of everything is, it is not as bad as that random element.

Just to show you how invasive this process is, I'll tell you what I'm thinking right now: *Do I want to save this? Is it worth saving? What could come from this? Will this cause an uproar in an Arab state like that cartoon?* Geez, it never ends.

The Conscious Coma

Despite the bizarre title, I'm not crazy. I did mean to put "conscious" before the word "coma."

All my life there have been spans of time that stick out because of something that, before today, made them almost as if they never happened, or at least they felt like a dream. These spans could last for a day, a week, or longer; the longest one that I recognize lasted well over six months.

So what is this "conscious coma"? My definition is a state when a person (like me) becomes so self-absorbed that the outside world sort of fades away. During this time, the person's contact with the outside world will be minimal and utilitarian at best. To others, it may seem that the person has become dumb, uninterested, or just plain rude. It might look that way, but in reality the mind becomes so self-absorbed that it becomes nearly impossible to process external stimuli.

If one of these comas lasted forever, the person would

never really have to deal with reality because the perceived reality of the coma would be overpowering. Is this what full-blown autism is all about?

For me, though, there are awakenings, and every time these happen, all the stress and bad things that have happened since the previous awakening flood in at light speed. To make an analogy, it is sort of like a family that goes on vacation and doesn't ask anyone to pick up their mail. A day goes by, then a week, and then finally a month (long vacation). When the family gets back, the amount of mail to go through will be overwhelming.

The best example of this coma happened back in June of 2004. Six months prior, I had broken up with Emily for the last time. On this June day I was working a practice session at the racetrack. One of the drivers asked me if I'd take his kart out to give him some setup advice. I happily agreed, and within fifteen minutes I was suited up and on the track. After about six laps, I had an awakening.

Going into the third turn, the left rear tire decided it would abandon the other three. Turn three is a fast right-hander, and the left rear is a very important tire for that turn. As the tire came off, I went into an immediate snap spin that nearly rolled the kart. While spinning, I was also nearly hit by three other karts on track. During the spin, I awoke. The chain of thought was like this: *Boy, I can't wait to tell Emily this. Wait a sec, Emily? Emily? I don't think I talk to her anymore. Why don't I? What happened? I think I broke up with her. Oh my goodness; it's June! Where did the last six months go!*

I do remember those months, but while spinning, it was

as if all the bad stuff was experienced for the first time. Compared to the vacuum that sucked my breath away as a result of the pain of suffering from all the things that happened over the last six months, the physical forces of the spin were nothing.

That's the story side of it, but there's more to describe as to what it is like while in this conscious coma.

While in this state, as I've said, emotions are on delay. It is a horrible feeling for me because I know I should feel something about any given situation, but nothing is there. The feelings are on hold, much like being recorded on a DVR for viewing later.

While in this conscious coma, the ability to cope with variables and lots of people drops. My mind is on such hyper-focus that it is like a person on a very thin balance beam on a windy day and all it will take to knock the guy off is just one gust of wind. This could explain why I broke up with Emily a dozen times only to call back the next day expecting things to be normal. If she knocked me off track in my thinking, the automated response, regardless of whom or what it is, is to cut it off or shut it out so I can be whole again in my thoughts.

This has been one of the hardest things I've written because it is so deep and mysterious. I'm only starting to understand this, and I never would have discovered it had I not been thinking deeply about why I experience such contrast in my conscious world. Could this be the tip of the iceberg on fully understanding Asperger's?

Invisible Reminders

As I've written many times before, my mind is constantly thinking about everything. While awake there is no escape from my mind's constant scanning and calculating. With that being said, it would seem sleep would be the refuge from the chaotic thinking, but it is not so.

Since I always go upon the assumption that if it happens to me it's the way it is for all, I never gave this topic much thought. For me, dreams are nothing more than an extension of consciousness. Every night I will remember all my dreams in the sequence they occurred. Up until about two months ago, I thought this was so for everybody, but that was until a person looked at me as if I had told them that I was a ghost.

As successful as my mind is at creating stress while I am awake, it's even better while I'm asleep. The reason it's so good at stirring up trouble is the fact that I am fully aware during my dreams, and to make this sound even more false, I am able to be aware of the fact that I am dreaming.

A few years back, when I was in the midst of my breakup with Linda, I had a recurring dream. After a couple of nights, each time the dream would start I would know the plot. It was sort of like watching a rerun on television, knowing what's going to happen. In those dreams I was able to interact differently with the cast of characters, but the end result was almost the same each time.

It's quite odd to be able to act like myself completely in my dreams, yet be aware that it is, in fact, a dream. Maybe this power, or rather awareness, has prevented nightmares. I can't remember having a nightmare like other people describe. Yes, bad things happen to me (I, for some reason, am constantly being electrocuted in my dreams by AM radio towers. I know, I know, I'm odd), but it is never scary. I would take nightmares, though, instead of the pain that dreams cause.

If something is troubling me, I will probably dream about it. The dream would go along the plotline of trying to figure out all the possibilities and possible solutions to the problem. I may be aware of the dream, but I turn the television off, so to speak. If I'm awake, I do have the chance of diverting my attention, but while asleep my mind is able to do what it pleases. That being so, the reminders of what are, what was, and what will never be can't be blocked.

To let you know how aware I am in my dreams, I'll tell you about a dream I had last night. The location was a level from the game *Halo*, and for some reason there was a concert there. Before the concert began, I was worrying about things in the real world and at the same time thinking about strategies to use next time I play that level. Right before the concert was to commence I was, for no apparent reason, attacked by a tiger shark. My conscious mind immediately pointed out that this could not happen because there was no water. I got quite annoyed because it kept biting my hand, and I was trying to tell myself that this was completely false, but it just kept trying to eat my hand. Because of this fact, I started thinking about sharks and then made a mental note to check the Internet for facts about tiger sharks.

Every night is like that, to some extent. To further the incredible nature of this, I'll point out that as the night progresses, I am aware, to a certain degree, of how much longer I can sleep. I can do this because as the time to wake approaches, my dreams become even more vivid. They become so vivid that sometimes I can't tell the difference between reality and the dream. As becoming awake nears, my dreams shift into a pattern of planning the day's activities. The first thing I do every morning is to call my dad just to see if anything is new. I'll dream about this before I do it, and sometimes when I wake I will have the thought that I had already called him several times.

A couple of months ago I had a dream about losing money while playing blackjack. I thought this was true for many days until I checked my checkbook and what I dreamed about wasn't there.

Before you get envious about me being able to recall dreams, you should know it's a curse. As I said earlier, my dreams tell me what is, what was, and what will never be. Imagine someone giving you one of those prank lottery tickets and you think you've won a million dollars and then you find out it's merely a joke. I live this every night! Every night I'm normal, only to reenter this realm where all is not well.

I don't fear going to sleep at all, but I always dread what the morning will be like. I have no idea what I'll be reminded of and what will be cruelly taken away by simply waking up.

Quest

There's one topic that I have talked about several times but have never had a definitive answer on. I think this topic is a main theme, and for me it is very confusing. This topic is near and dear to everyone, and everyone probably has a different opinion on it, but for me I am clueless to what it even is. That topic is love.

Unknowingly, I started a quest when I began writing to try to learn what love is. What does "I love you" mean? If I don't know the meaning, am I able to love? We are bombarded each day by thousands of sources (primarily media outlets) telling us what love is. In movies, I'm sure the concept works on people, but that assumes that they understand the concept. I don't think I do.

Anything that happens with me internally is to the extreme. I either feel very strongly for or very strongly against something. However, with emotions I'm either content or extremely upset. There is nothing I know past content on the positive side. Does this mean I am incapable of love, or do I have to be content with being content?

Of all the things I am shorthanded on, the one I truly feel sad about is this lack of understanding of the concept of love. As I've said before, the only thing I know about love is that I'd miss a person if they were gone. I truly hate that sentence, but that's all I know. Of all the inner rage I have, the majority is directed toward this enigma, this unknown emotion shrouded in mystery.

Without knowledge of what it really is, I fear I may get caught up in a horrible relationship. You see, when talking to someone, I get caught up in a tsunami of sorts. I may not like what's being said, but because I can't change a situation I just give the answer of least resistance, so the tsunami rolls on.

Now, what if I have loved, but it's simply so overwhelming that I didn't even know it? Say, like a circuit breaking? What if it was so perfect that it was unbearable? This could be, but I'd be scared if this is true because then the first, according to theory, could not be duplicated.

But what about family? There should be something there, right? Again, I hate this. I absolutely hate this. In any situation, I can only think how the outcome will affect me. Call it selfish if you want, but I am unable to feel any emotion about another person.

My mom is constantly bugging me to see her since she lives about a thousand miles away. Last New Year's, I drove up to Indianapolis to see her. It had been more than a year since we had last met. She was excited to see me, but I was impartial. You see, to love is to be bound by time. If my mind thinks differently in regards to memories, then for her it's been a year but for me it's been just another day. The same thing will probably happen this year as well, and I'm sure she'll get misty-eyed and I again will be impartial.

Can love and time coincide? To love someone is to look forward to the future, but what if all I can see is what was? Does this mean I do in fact love, but only in the past? Can I only love what was and not what is or what's to come? I wish I could say how tragic not even knowing this is for me.

There is one love I do understand. It's a perfect love—so simple, so true. It's the love of an animal. With the wonderful animals I have had, there's no doubt what love is. With a pet there are no hidden strings, and by mere observation I can deduce what the mood of the animal is. This topic is so overwhelming that it's almost impossible to write about it. With an animal, there is never a feeling of aloneness. The fear of the open-ended situation is nonexistent; therefore, my mind doesn't overthink and I can simply enjoy the company of the animal.

Could it be there is no such thing as love among humans, and I'm the only one who realizes it? What if the term is just thrown around to make sense of an otherwise chaotic and strange world? Could it be that the world, in general, uses every other person and that love is just a myth? I surely hope not, because that would make the world all the scarier.

As you can see, I have plenty of questions and few answers. The quest will certainly continue. Where the destination is, I don't know. Is there more beyond "I'd miss you if you were gone"? I've done so much in my life, but I'd trade it all in a heartbeat to know what love is, even if it's just for a second, because with my memory, that second would last a lifetime.

Tomorrow Is an Eternity Away

During a routine conversation recently, it struck me that for me time is different. The conversation was about school and how something would take *only* two years. This thought made me really uncomfortable and almost angry. It wasn't the thought of going to school for two years, but just the thought of time itself.

My memory is such that it seems everything in my life happened within the past day. This makes my life seem like the present and past are just a split second. This, however, compromises the future, because I have no time perception. So if my entire life took only an hour, then how many events will take place within a year?

Quite an interesting concept, I believe. Is this the reason the concept of years of schooling sends bolts of anger through my veins? It isn't the actual time of being at school that makes me mad, but rather the complete absence of the concept of time. This isn't to say that an actual year goes by slowly for me. I am constantly thinking that actual time isn't as far ahead as it actually is (it's nearly July already?!). However, to say now that something will take four months creates panic and fear.

There are two things going on here. First is the lack of perception; second, if something is going to take place in the future, then I'll have all that time to think about it. I am in a constant state of thought, and prolonged thought on an individual idea isn't a good thing, so when there's this long-term goal or destination, it's a guaranteed X amount of time that I know I'll be thinking about whatever it is.

This lack of perception, though, may be where the true problem lies. Perception is everything. Without depth perception, many routine tasks are impossible. With this time perception, it feels as if my entire past has been a couple of minutes, but the future is an eternity away. The saying is that time heals all wounds, but what if I am incapable of putting that time in between any given event and me? Could this be the true reason that I am stuck in the past? Well, rather, the recently perceived past?

This is how I can recall names, events, and minor details that no one else would remember. I must drive people crazy correcting them on what they said and the order they said it when talking about a conversation from five years ago. For me it's easy, because we *just* had the conversation. For them, however, it's been those five years, and who in their right mind remembers something that took place that long ago?

If the past never really became the past, what would hap-

pen in the mind? There could never be anything that could
be "let go," so to speak. Friends lost would stay lost and the
initial grief would remain. The time spent away from others
would seem like a second when it could be a day, month, or
year.

Once again, it is almost hurting my mind trying to verbalize this. I know it's a key topic, and I feel that it is the
cause of a lot of issues. Can they be resolved, though? I hate
to say this, but only time will tell, and that time, whatever
it may be, scares me.

If I Were Dying of Thirst . . .
Would I Ask for a Glass of Water?

If a person wanted something so badly it hurt, logic would say that they would ask for it. Ask and you shall receive— but what if asking were virtually impossible?

Recently I directed a race in Iowa. It was a very eye-opening trip for me because I learned a lot about myself and raised a lot of questions about why I do the things I do.

The race weekend was not what I was used to. The track owners had a very "hands-on" approach, and they were the ones who really ran the show. On Sunday, I found out that they had a flagman. If I were to say that I wanted to maintain my position with the race series, I would break the heart of their longtime flagman because there had not been a big race at that track for nearly half a decade. This tore me in two.

About the only thing I look forward to in life right now is to be the flagman; now I was put in an unfair position. If I said no to the old man, that would be taking away what may or may not be the only thing that *he* looks forward to. Furthermore, it would make me look like a jerk and then the rest of the day the track crew would be most unhelpful if I needed them. Because of this, I allowed the old man to flag.

The track owner took over the duties of race director. I was still on the track, and ultimately handled decisions on protests and such, but instead of being the most recognized figure on the track I was behind the curtains, so to speak. I guess you'd compare it to a football coach being moved to the general manager. Perhaps it's a move up, but the instant choices of plays are now out of the hands of the former coach. I know if I do the job, it will be done right, but at that track I was like a general manager who only got to handle the aftermath and not the actual game.

Because of all this, it was most obvious to those who see me at our track that I was a bit flustered. "Smile, Aaron," I heard a couple of people say. I still had one bright spot; I was scheduled to race in the TaG Senior final. (TaG stands for "Touch and Go" and refers to a kart with an onboard starter.) As the day's luck would have it, though, that opportunity went away as well. Greg, the kart shop owner I work for, has a "Rent and Ride" program. The kart I was to drive was rented. He said he'd try to find a replacement, but I said no. Looking back, I don't know why I declined the offer. After no replacement was found, he said that at the end of the day I could take out the "rented" kart out for as long as I wanted.

That glimmer of hope got me through the day, and I

looked forward to getting behind the wheel again. The day came to a close and I returned to the pits, and since the awards ceremonies were over the karts were being loaded into the trailer. I helped, knowing that when they went in there would be no chance of me getting the track time I so badly yearned for.

The karts were loaded, and eight hours later sitting at a bar with Greg, he finally remembered that he forgot to let me get on the track. I just nodded my head and went back to watching the television. Then he asked me why I didn't remind him. My mind instantly locked up. I responded with something along the lines that I simply can't ask for things. This was the answer of least resistance, but it turns out to be true. I live for the moments behind the wheel; they are what keep the next day of life worth living, and on that day I could have had that chance, but as powerful as the need to drive is, it doesn't surpass the inability to remind a person of something they had said earlier. Racing is very much like water for me in that it is required. I had a big pitcher of water lined up, but I was unable to ask him to hand it to me after he already promised it.

If something were already promised, then why would reminding a person about it be impossible for me? I figured at the time that because it was the only thing I was thinking about, how could he forget it? I thought that my appearance in the pit would be enough to remind him, but it wasn't. As I stood in the pits, he saw me. I instantly came to no less than a hundred conclusions as to why I would not be able to drive. Was he mad? If so, was it at me? Why would he be?

Was it broken? Question after question filled my mind. Of all the questions, though, the most obvious one was never considered: "Did he forget?"

If I can't predict the answer, or at least be pretty certain, I won't ask the question. In everyday life, most questions can be answered with a yes or no. Those are only two answers, but there'd be at least fifty reasons a person would say yes or no, and with so many possibilities it becomes impossible to know what the answer is and *why* the answer is what it is, and therefore no question can be asked. I had a chance to be alive again, but I remained silent.

I realize this does not make sense. However, I live in a world where I can't vocalize what I need. Be it anything in the world, whether it's the go-kart incident, or if I want to stop for food, or any other question that involves me, I will most likely be unable to ask for it. There are certain situations where I am able to, but as a general rule, I cannot.

As I think about this, I realize that this, too, is a major cause of internal strife. I wonder how many opportunities I've missed just because I was unable to answer the knock at the door because I was unable to ask, "Who's there?"

The Limit of "Coulds"

With the inabilities I have, my anxiety level is over-the-top. For instance, right now one "could" is, "Will I ever race professionally?" If I did race, *could* life be bearable? For me, right now, that "could" is paralyzing.

Being at the limit of my tolerance level can be compared to that one drop of water that overflows a glass. Using water is a bad example. Let's say that drop is gasoline and below the glass is an open flame. In this example, one drop *could* create quite the problem.

What exactly is the problem, though? I worry about money and I worry about my racing career. If I have no money at all, I am at peace. That's because there is no "could." "Could I run out of money?" has already been answered. It isn't the "is" that creates the problems but the "coulds" that could kill.

Of all things it was my old fear of thunderstorms that truly made this clear. When I was younger, storms were crippling for me. However, when a storm came, there was no issue. It wasn't the storm itself that created the fear but rather the "*Could* this be the worst storm ever?" A thunderstorm *could* last for fifteen minutes. Imagine the stress of something that has many more "coulds" and lasts for weeks or months. When my glass overflows and the fire is lit, everything becomes hopeless. The ability to tolerate minuscule events becomes nonexistent. I believe this is a problem for a lot of people on the spectrum. To create a stable environment, the number of "coulds" needs to be reduced. How is this done? Sadly, I don't think it'll be easy. But the simple fact of recognizing this problem *could* reduce some of the anxiety. With the anxiety produced by these "coulds" comes the further anxiety of "*Could* this anxiety keep up? *Could* there be more?" You see the problem.

I think people have realized that it's the gray area of things that people like me have trouble with. I think I have given this gray area a name, "the Coulds," and I hope this helps others realize the true scope of the matter.

I wonder if this could be true?

Asperger's Geometry

Of all places to have a revelation, I didn't think jury duty would be one of them. But recently it was.

As I was doing crossword puzzles waiting for the courtroom to open, I overheard the people in front of me talking about bowling. Since bowling is Kansas material for me, I started listening. There were three ladies talking and two were avid bowlers. The third bowled, but she knew somebody who was a diehard bowler. She said this person, a coworker at the St. Louis Bread Company, had been bowling since the age of five and currently bowled on two leagues. My heart immediately sank.

I probably should've gone right back to my crossword puzzle, but I had to eliminate the possible "coulds," so I asked, "I take it you work at the Sunset Hills Bread Company and you're talking about Emily." The lady looked very perplexed, as if I were somehow a psychic. She nodded that I was right. I then mentioned that I was her boyfriend for nearly four years. Her response was devastating: "Oh yes, I've heard about you."

Heard about me? The number of things this *could* mean became infinite.

This concept got me thinking, and it's very much like geometry. Let's say someone meets the person they marry on day X. Day X becomes the start of a ray. A ray is a line that starts at a given point and extends in one direction forever. Now let's say they get a divorce. Then what had been a ray, going forever in one direction, becomes a line segment, point A to point B, with a beginning and an end.

Those two examples are what apply to normal people. As usual, the norm doesn't fit me. For me, when anything major happens, it instantly becomes a line. A line in geometry is a line that stretches infinitely in two directions. With that being so, I would ask you to try to find the start and end of the mentioned line. It'd be like trying to find the start of the equator. As confusing for you as it might be to accomplish the mentioned task, it is even harder for me. Why? As with all of my examples, the lines represent life. Now, when the proverbial couple gets married, their ray stretches out toward the future with a defined start.

It's been two years since I last heard Emily's voice. A friend, if I had any, might say it's time to move on. That would be great advice, but since my mind cannot perceive a defined start or end, it can't "move on" because it always is in an infinite state of being.

Questions such as: "Who has Emily become?" "What has she seen?" and "Is she happy?" will probably always haunt me. The tragic thing that happened at jury duty was that I was going to possibly get some answers, but just after she confirmed that the person she was talking about was Emily, and after she said she heard about me, the bailiff came out and it was time to enter the courtroom. Further, adding to the sheer tragedy of it all, she was picked for the jury and I wasn't, thus ending any hope of hearing anything more.

I never realized in grade school that geometry would come in handy. What I also didn't realize was the complexity of it. On paper it seems so benign. Lines going this way, rays going that way, an intersection here, but when you start to think about it and those lines become life, well, perhaps I should have paid more attention in geometry so I know how it all ends.

The Fourth Wall

When you attend a live play, you are watching a preset production and script in progress. Normally, during a play, the audience has no say in what occurs onstage; it is all predetermined. I don't think any Shakespearean play has any characters asking audience members how they should respond to any given dilemma. Imagine how you would respond if you were sitting in the front row and the title character breaks the norm and asks you directly how they should proceed. If they were to do this, that would be an example of a breach of the fourth wall—that is, the imaginary wall in front of the stage that audience members view through.

The question is, though, how would you respond? Let's say you've been to a hundred plays and know every line, but then for some odd reason you are suddenly part of the play. Even if you knew what they should do in accordance with the script, I'm sure you would be frozen. This is how every day is for me. As I see life move about around me, I take the role of an audience member. I hope to be nothing more than a dark figure in a dimly lit room, simply viewing the proceedings of the world. As William Shakespeare said, "All the world's a stage." He probably had Asperger's, because it is true.

There are a lot of postmodern plays that purposely break the fourth wall, but it's merely the character talking to the audience without the response altering the course of the production. Those who frequent plays would grow accustomed to this. I, however, am not able to make that transition in life to get used to myself becoming part of the production. In this instance, the production is life itself.

Perhaps this is why smaller groups are preferable, because the fewer people there are, the better the chances that some random act won't propel me into the production. There is an exception to this, though, as I just realized; as long as I am the sole performer of any given act in life, there is no issue. Successful one-person plays are far and few between.

One would have to think that a person could grow accustomed to becoming part of the production, but there's literally a wall preventing it, not the fourth wall, but let's say the fifth wall that would be called a mental wall.

The more I think about this, the more it really sells the point. In all my memories, I always remember myself as an invisible observer of events unfolding around me, and I like it that way. As long as I'm not seen, there will be safety because I won't have to become part of the act.

Life doesn't have a script, but there are guidelines to

how a play will go. Guidelines aren't rules. Therefore, they are the gray areas of life. If that is so, then how can I know how to act? My actions will affect the play going on around me, but how can I minimize the damage since I am merely a simple observer? There's an issue with the answer, though. The easy answer is to stay home or find a hole to crawl into, but at the same time, while the play of life goes on around me, I have my own production of life going on.

It's a fine line, but one that has to be balanced. As much as I want to, staying home forever is not an option. The fourth wall will be breached, shattered, and stomped on every day that I live, and the fifth wall will prevent me from fully responding. But as they say, the show must go on, and therefore so will I.

Aliases

Personally, I have been baffled by my ability to do certain things. Some people are unable to talk in front of a large audience, but I can. When working in retail I could sell stuff to people who may or may not want whatever it was I was selling, and I was phenomenal at it.

I have wondered deeply how or why I am able to do this because a few people have said that I should be unable to. I have hinted before that the reason I am able to is the "Game Theory" I wrote about. While that theory is still true in my mind, I believe it goes much deeper than I thought. To work to its fullest extent, the game must have me doing something that isn't me completely; enter the alias element.

When I am directing races I am not completely myself; if I ask someone to do something, it isn't me asking but rather the race director. Yes, I may be the race director, but it isn't me who's asking. Confused? Let me explain more.

When I worked at the video game store and I was up-selling unsuspecting customers, it wasn't me doing the selling but the easy-to-like, "I'm on your side" salesperson I portrayed. If I were to have talked to that customer outside the store at the end of my shift, I could not ask a single question because then it would be me asking and then there is no protection. That's the important thing when in alias mode; there is safety in the fact that I am only whom I portray. When the protection isn't there, though, getting knocked out of Kansas is alarmingly close.

Let's take an example that happened at a race I was in recently. Earlier in the weekend, the team owner asked me if I could get some gas for one of his karts. To let you know, I am currently working at this owner's kart shop, so that made the alias factor easy because I could go to his customers not as myself but as the data-entry salesperson that I am. Two days after that, though, it was my turn to need fuel, and this eliminated any and all aliases from the equation. I could not be the salesperson because it was *me* who needed it.

This was just a horrible situation. The crisis at hand could not have been worse because on one side there's racing, which trumps all, and on the flip side was me having to leave Kansas.

What did I do? I decided not to race. I didn't want to be in the way, as I was six seconds off the pace, but when I told Greg, the shop owner, he started berating me with the same response I'd give someone in my position—that it's the overtaking kart's responsibility to overtake cleanly. I knew I had no logical counterpoints to this, and when Greg said that I can't let fear dictate what I do, I then mentioned, "Well, I don't have fuel, though." I don't know if he understood at that point in time if the whole debacle was just because I couldn't ask someone else for help. Whether he knew then or knows now makes no difference. For the first time in my life, racing lost.

The important fact here is that when I'm acting as someone else, the state lines of all other states around Kansas are very far away. So long as I am not myself, life is fine. What I find fascinating is the fact that this doesn't work in reverse. I could ask that almighty question of, "Sir, can I help you find anything today?" but if *I* am asked that, I lock up.

Certainly this is a hard concept to grasp because it truly is a difference of staggering proportions. I think people who see me in both areas will clearly understand this, but if a person has seen me only at the track, then they probably think of me as a very confident person with no fear of talking to people. If only they knew the truth. The few people I have let know the truth thought I was joking at first. This means my covert op works great. People who see me outside the tracks, though, when told that I speak in front of two hundred people, think that I am just making this up.

I will give myself credit somewhat in that, even if it is an alias, it is still me. If I weren't internally strong enough, there is no way this would be possible. This is a conduit I use to, perhaps, let the real me show through momentarily. If I have to portray something else to show my true self, then so be it. I just hope there are enough games and roles in the future so I can, from time to time, be as close to normal as I can possibly be.

In the End

With writing more than a year now on my experiences and thoughts regarding Asperger's, I feel it is proper to write a final chapter. I write this in the same room I wrote "Scream" and "School" some nineteen months ago. This room is room number 312 in the Imperial Hotel in Kisumu, Kenya. This is a fitting place to write my final chapter, because it was in this very room that I first thought that my writings may actually be used for something. From that point on, I took my insights very seriously.

So with all that I have written, what have I learned? I have come to understand for one that I am, indeed, different. It's not that radically different, though, but just a different understanding of the world.

I have learned that I am very lucky to have such great parents who allowed me to be me. I have realized that I have had many experiences that "normal" people will never have. I believe that both of those things have allowed me to write this material.

It's interesting to think that the start of my writings came about because of the end of a relationship. When I lost touch with Emily for the last time, after she said something along the lines of "You have Asperger's. Why would I want to know you?" I wrote her a letter. Then I kept going. I wrote about Linda, my first relationship, and then I started thinking about other things to write about and it snowballed from there. It was very much like the scene in the movie *Forrest Gump*, when Forrest starts running and he gets to the county line and he just keeps going for the sake of going. What started out as a means of sharing my story as an act of childish revenge grew into the opportunity to hopefully change other people's lives. Because of this, I can do nothing but thank Emily for inadvertently unlocking these ideas. I believe that my "Quest" has come to an end. I do believe that only the shock of a deep love lost could have inspired me to write them down.

Finally, I have learned that Asperger's isn't the end of the world. I've heard stories from parents who freaked when they learned that their child had it. I was a bit spooked when I learned I had it, but now, yes, now, I am thankful I have it. Because of it, I lead a life I can be proud of. I don't drink, smoke, party, have fun (wait a sec—I have fun), or do other lewd stuff that may show up on a police report fifteen years from now. It allows me to act older than my age, and this has allowed me to do so many things at such a young age. I know that not all those affected will be as fortunate as me, but there can be a prosperous life. There is still much to be learned about it, and I will continue to think and write because I realize that I have only scratched the tip of the iceberg.

ABOUT THE AUTHOR

© 1998, James Likens

Aaron Likens was born on February 4, 1983, in Scottsbluff, Nebraska, and spent most of his childhood in Indianapolis, where he and his father spent many afternoons at the Indianapolis Motor Speedway watching practice for the Indy 500. Somewhere around age four, Aaron decided he wanted to be a race car driver. The desire has never left.

The family moved to St. Louis, Missouri, in 1993, and in 1995, Aaron began racing go-karts. Shortly after that he became the starter/flagman for the St. Louis Karting Association. Diagnosed with Asperger's syndrome in 2004, Aaron began writing essays so that he wouldn't have to talk with those at the Judevine Center who diagnosed him.

While he still looks forward to racing, he sees his current mission in life to speak to families, educators, clinicians, and others about his experience with Asperger's.

Visit his blog at AaronLikens.com and his website at Finding Kansas.com.